MOS 2013 Study Guide
for Microsoft Excel

Joan Lambert

PUBLISHED BY
Microsoft Press
A Division of Microsoft Corporation
One Microsoft Way
Redmond, Washington 98052-6399

Library of Congress Control Number: 2013939519
ISBN: 978-0-7356-6920-8

Printed and bound in the United States of America.

Fifth Printing: July 2015

Microsoft Press books are available through booksellers and distributors worldwide. If you need support related to this book, email Microsoft Press Book Support at mspinput@microsoft.com. Please tell us what you think of this book at http://www.microsoft.com/learning/booksurvey.

Acquisitions Editor: Rosemary Caperton
Editorial Production: Online Training Solutions, Inc. (OTSI)
Technical Reviewer: Rob Carr (OTSI)
Copyeditor: Jaime Odell (OTSI)
Indexer: Krista Wall (OTSI)
Cover: Microsoft Press Brand Team

Contents

What do you think of this book? We want to hear from you!

Microsoft is interested in hearing your feedback so we can continually improve our books and learning resources for you. To participate in a brief online survey, please visit:

microsoft.com/learning/booksurvey

What do you think of this book? We want to hear from you!

Microsoft is interested in hearing your feedback so we can continually improve our books and learning resources for you. To participate in a brief online survey, please visit:

microsoft.com/learning/booksurvey

Introduction

The Microsoft Office Specialist (MOS) certification program has been designed to validate your knowledge of and ability to use programs in the Microsoft Office 2013 suite of programs, Microsoft Office 365, and Microsoft SharePoint. This book has been designed to guide you in studying the types of tasks you are likely to be required to demonstrate in Exam 77-420: Microsoft Excel 2013.

> **See Also** For information about the tasks you are likely to be required to demonstrate in Exams 77-427 and 77-428: Microsoft Excel 2013 Expert, see *MOS 2013 Study Guide for Microsoft Excel Expert* by Mark Dodge (Microsoft Press, 2013).

Who this book is for

MOS 2013 Study Guide for Microsoft Excel is designed for experienced computer users seeking Microsoft Office Specialist certification in Excel 2013.

MOS exams for individual programs are practical rather than theoretical. You must demonstrate that you can complete certain tasks or projects rather than simply answering questions about program features. The successful MOS certification candidate will have at least six months of experience using all aspects of the application on a regular basis; for example, using Excel at work or school to create and manage workbooks and worksheets, modify and format cell content, present data in tables and charts, perform calculations on data, and insert and format objects in a worksheet.

As a certification candidate, you probably have a lot of experience with the program you want to become certified in. Many of the procedures described in this book will be familiar to you; others might not be. Read through each study section and ensure that you are familiar with not only the procedures included in the section, but also the concepts and tools discussed in the review information. In some cases, graphics depict the tools you will use to perform procedures related to the skill set. Study the graphics and ensure that you are familiar with all the options available for each tool.

How this book is organized

The exam coverage is divided into chapters representing broad skill sets that correlate to the functional groups covered by the exam, and each chapter is divided into sections addressing groups of related skills that correlate to the exam objectives. Each section includes review information, generic procedures, and practice tasks you can complete on your own while studying. When necessary, we provide practice files you can use to work through the practice tasks. You can practice the procedures in this book by using the practice files supplied or by using your own files.

Throughout this book, you will find Strategy tips that present information about the scope of study that is necessary to ensure that you achieve mastery of a skill set and are successful in your certification effort.

Download the practice files

Before you can complete the practice tasks in this book, you need to download the book's practice files to your computer. These practice files can be downloaded from the following page:

http://aka.ms/mosExcel2013/files

> **Important** The Excel 2013 program is not available from this website. You should purchase and install that program before using this book.

If you would like to be able to refer to the completed versions of practice files at a later time, you can save the practice files that you modify while working through the exercises in this book. If you save your changes and later want to repeat the exercise, you can download the original practice files again. The following table lists the practice files for this book.

Folder and chapter	Files
MOSExcel2013\Objective1	*Excel_1-1.xlsx*
1 Create and manage workbooks and worksheets	*Excel_1-2a.xlsx*
	Excel_1-2b.xlsx
	Excel_1-3a.xlsx
	Excel_1-3b.xlsx
	Excel_1-3c.xlsx
	Excel_1-3d.xlsx

Folder and chapter	Files
MOSExcel2013\Objective1 *(continued)*	*Excel_1-4a.xlsx*
1 Create and manage workbooks and worksheets	*Excel_1-4b.xlsx*
	Excel_1-4c.xlsx
	Excel_1-5a.xlsx
	Excel_1-5b.xlsm
MOSExcel2013\Objective2	*Excel_2-1a.xlsx*
2 Manage cells and ranges	*Excel_2-1b.xlsx*
	Excel_2-1c.xlsx
	Excel_2-1d.xlsx
	Excel_2-2a.xlsx
	Excel_2-2b.xlsx
	Excel_2-3a.xlsx
	Excel_2-3b.xlsx
	Excel_2-3c.xlsx
	Excel_2-3d.xlsx
	Excel_2-3e.xlsx
MOSExcel2013\Objective3	*Excel_3-1.xlsx*
3 Manage tables	*Excel_3-2.xlsx*
	Excel_3-3a.xlsx
	Excel_3-3b.xlsx
MOSExcel2013\Objective4	*Excel_4-1a.xlsx*
4 Apply formulas and functions	*Excel_4-1b.xlsx*
	Excel_4-1c.xlsx
	Excel_4-2a.xlsx
	Excel_4-2b.xlsx
	Excel_4-3.xlsx
	Excel_4-4.xlsx
MOSExcel2013\Objective5	*Excel_5-1a.xlsx*
5 Create charts and objects	*Excel_5-1b.xlsx*
	Excel_5-1c.xlsx
	Excel_5-2a.xlsx
	Excel_5-2b.xlsx
	Excel_5-2c.xlsx
	Excel_5-3a.xlsx
	Excel_5-3b.png
	Excel_5-3c.txt
	Excel_5-3d.jpg

Adapting exercise steps

The screen images shown in this book were captured at a screen resolution of 1024 × 768, at 100 percent magnification. If your settings are different, the ribbon on your screen might not look the same as the one shown in this book. For example, you might have more or fewer buttons in each of the groups, the buttons you have might be represented by larger or smaller icons than those shown, or the group might be represented by a button that you click to display the group's commands. As a result, exercise instructions that involve the ribbon might require a little adaptation. Our instructions use this format:

➜ On the **Insert** tab, in the **Illustrations** group, click the **Chart** button.

If the command is in a list or on a menu, our instructions use this format:

➜ On the **Home** tab, in the **Editing** group, click the **Find** arrow and then, on the **Find** menu, click **Advanced Find**.

> **Tip** On subsequent instances of instructions located on the same tab or in the same group, the instructions are simplified to reflect that we've already established the working location.

If differences between your display settings and ours cause a button to appear differently on your screen than it does in this book, you can easily adapt the steps to locate the command. First click the specified tab, and then locate the specified group. If a group has been collapsed into a group list or under a group button, click the list or button to display the group's commands. If you can't immediately identify the button you want, point to likely candidates to display their names in ScreenTips.

If you prefer not to have to adapt the steps, set up your screen to match ours while you read and work through the exercises in this book.

In this book, we provide instructions based on the traditional keyboard and mouse input methods. If you're using the program on a touch-enabled device, you might be giving commands by tapping with a stylus or your finger. If so, substitute a tapping action any time we instruct you to click a user interface element. Also note that when we tell you to enter information, you can do so by typing on a keyboard, tapping an on-screen keyboard, or even speaking aloud, depending on your computer setup and your personal preferences.

Get support and give feedback

The following sections provide information about getting help with this book and contacting us to provide feedback or report errors.

Errata

We've made every effort to ensure the accuracy of this book and its companion content. Any errors that have been reported since this book was published are listed on our Microsoft Press site:

http://aka.ms/mosExcel2013/errata

If you find an error that is not already listed, you can report it to us through the same page.

If you need additional support, send an email message to Microsoft Press Book Support at:

mspinput@microsoft.com

Please note that product support for Microsoft software is not offered through the preceding addresses.

We want to hear from you

At Microsoft Press, your satisfaction is our top priority, and your feedback our most valuable asset. Please tell us what you think of this book at:

http://www.microsoft.com/learning/booksurvey

The survey is short, and we read every one of your comments and ideas. Thanks in advance for your input!

Stay in touch

Let's keep the conversation going! We're on Twitter at:

http://twitter.com/MicrosoftPress

Taking a Microsoft Office Specialist exam

Desktop computing proficiency is increasingly important in today's business world. When screening, hiring, and training employees, employers can feel reassured by relying on the objectivity and consistency of technology certification to ensure the competence of their workforce. As an employee or job seeker, you can use technology certification to prove that you already have the skills you need to succeed, saving current and future employers the time and expense of training you.

Microsoft Office Specialist certification

Microsoft Office Specialist certification is designed to assist employees in validating their skills with Office programs. The following certification paths are available:

- A **Microsoft Office Specialist (MOS)** is an individual who has demonstrated proficiency by passing a certification exam in one or more Office programs, including Microsoft Word, Excel, PowerPoint, Outlook, Access, OneNote, or SharePoint.

- A **Microsoft Office Specialist Expert (MOS Expert)** is an individual who has taken his or her knowledge of Office to the next level and has demonstrated by passing a certification exam that he or she has mastered the more advanced features of Word or Excel.

Selecting a certification path

When deciding which certifications you would like to pursue, you should assess the following:

- The program and program version(s) with which you are familiar
- The length of time you have used the program and how frequently you use it
- Whether you have had formal or informal training in the use of that program
- Whether you use most or all of the available program features
- Whether you are considered a go-to resource by business associates, friends, and family members who have difficulty with the program

Candidates for MOS-level certification are expected to successfully complete a wide range of standard business tasks, such as formatting a document or worksheet and its content; creating and formatting visual content; or working with SharePoint lists, libraries, Web Parts, and dashboards. Successful candidates generally have six or more months of experience with the specific Office program, including either formal, instructor-led training or self-study using MOS-approved books, guides, or interactive computer-based materials.

Candidates for MOS Expert–level certification are expected to successfully complete more complex tasks that involve using the advanced functionality of the program. Successful candidates generally have at least six months, and might have several years, of experience with the programs, including formal, instructor-led training or self-study using MOS-approved materials.

Test-taking tips

Every MOS certification exam is developed from a set of exam skill standards (referred to as the objective domain) that are derived from studies of how the Office programs are used in the workplace. Because these skill standards dictate the scope of each exam, they provide critical information about how to prepare for certification. This book follows the structure of the published exam objectives; see "How this book is organized" in the Introduction for more information.

The MOS certification exams are performance based and require you to complete business-related tasks or projects in the program for which you are seeking certification. For example, you might be presented with a file and told to do something specific with it, or presented with a sample document and told to create it by using resources provided for that purpose. Your score on the exam reflects how well you perform the requested tasks or complete the project within the allotted time.

Here is some helpful information about taking the exam:

- Keep track of the time. Your exam time does not officially begin until after you finish reading the instructions provided at the beginning of the exam. During the exam, the amount of time remaining is shown at the bottom of the exam interface. You can't pause the exam after you start it.

- Pace yourself. At the beginning of the exam, you will receive information about the questions or projects that are included in the exam. Some questions will require that you complete more than one task. Each project will require that you complete multiple tasks. During the exam, the amount of time remaining to complete the questions or project, and the number of completed and remaining questions if applicable, is shown at the bottom of the exam interface.

- Read the exam instructions carefully before beginning. Follow all the instructions provided completely and accurately.

- Enter requested information as it appears in the instructions, but without duplicating the formatting unless you are specifically instructed to do so. For example, the text and values you are asked to enter might appear in the instructions in bold and underlined text, but you should enter the information without applying these formats.

- Close all dialog boxes before proceeding to the next exam question unless you are specifically instructed not to do so.

- Don't close task panes before proceeding to the next exam question unless you are specifically instructed to do so.

- If you are asked to print a document, worksheet, chart, report, or slide, perform the task, but be aware that nothing will actually be printed.

- When performing tasks to complete a project-based exam, save your work frequently.

- Don't worry about extra keystrokes or mouse clicks. Your work is scored based on its result, not on the method you use to achieve that result (unless a specific method is indicated in the instructions).

- If a computer problem occurs during the exam (for example, if the exam does not respond or the mouse no longer functions) or if a power outage occurs, contact a testing center administrator immediately. The administrator will restart the computer and return the exam to the point where the interruption occurred, with your score intact.

> **Strategy** This book includes special tips for effectively studying for the Microsoft Office Specialist exams in Strategy paragraphs such as this one.

Certification benefits

At the conclusion of the exam, you will receive a score report, indicating whether you passed the exam. If your score meets or exceeds the passing standard (the minimum required score), you will be contacted by email by the Microsoft Certification Program team. The email message you receive will include your Microsoft Certification ID and links to online resources, including the Microsoft Certified Professional site. On this site, you can download or order a printed certificate, create a virtual business card, order an ID card, view and share your certification transcript, access the Logo Builder, and access other useful and interesting resources, including special offers from Microsoft and affiliated companies.

Depending on the level of certification you achieve, you will qualify to display one of three logos on your business card and other personal promotional materials. These logos attest to the fact that you are proficient in the applications or cross-application skills necessary to achieve the certification.

Microsoft   **Microsoft**   **Microsoft**
Office Specialist   Office Specialist Expert   Office Specialist Master

Using the Logo Builder, you can create a personalized certification logo that includes the MOS logo and the specific programs in which you have achieved certification. If you achieve MOS certification in multiple programs, you can include multiple certifications in one logo.

For more information

To learn more about the Microsoft Office Specialist exams and related courseware, visit:

http://www.microsoft.com/learning/en/us/mos-certification.aspx

Microsoft Excel 2013

This book covers the skills you need to have for certification as a Microsoft Office Specialist in Microsoft Excel 2013. Specifically, you will need to be able to complete tasks that demonstrate the following skills:

1 Create and manage workbooks and worksheets

2 Manage cells and ranges

3 Create tables

4 Apply formulas and functions

5 Create charts and objects

With these skills, you can create, populate, format, and manage the types of workbooks and workbook content most commonly used in a business environment.

Prerequisites

We assume that you have been working with Excel 2013 for at least six months and that you know how to carry out fundamental tasks that are not specifically mentioned in the objectives for this Microsoft Office Specialist exam. Before you begin studying for this exam, you might want to make sure you are familiar with the information in this section.

Managing worksheets

➤ To delete a worksheet

→ Right-click the worksheet tab, and then click **Delete**.

→ With the worksheet active, on the **Home** tab, in the **Cells** group, click the **Delete** arrow, and then click **Delete Sheet**.

➤ To rename a worksheet

→ Double-click the worksheet tab, enter the new worksheet name, and then press **Enter**.

1. Right-click the worksheet tab, and then click **Rename**.

   Or

   On the **Home** tab, in the **Cells** group, click **Format**, and then in the **Organize Sheets** section, click **Rename Sheet**.

2. Enter the new worksheet name, and then press **Enter**.

Managing worksheet content

➤ To select all the content in a worksheet

→ At the junction of the row and column headings (above row 1 and to the left of column A), click the **Select All** button.

➤ To select an individual column or row

→ Click the column heading (labeled with the column letter) or the row heading (labeled with the row number).

Managing Excel tables

➤ To select data in a table, table column, or table row

→ Point to the upper-left corner of the table. When the pointer changes to a diagonal arrow, click once to select only the data, or twice to select the data and headers.

> **Tip** This method works only with tables, not with data ranges.

→ Point to the top edge of the table column. When the pointer changes to a downward-pointing arrow, click once to select only the data, or twice to select the data and header.

> **Tip** You must point to the edge of the table, not to the column heading or row heading.

→ Point to the left edge of the table row. When the pointer changes to a right-pointing arrow, click once to select the data.

Managing data entries

You enter text or a number in a cell simply by clicking the cell and entering the content. When entering content, a Cancel button (an X) and an Enter button (a check mark) are located between the formula bar and Name box, and the indicator at the left end of the status bar changes from Ready to Enter.

Excel allows a long text entry to overflow into an adjacent empty cell and truncates the entry only if the adjacent cell also contains an entry. However, unless you tell it otherwise, Excel displays long numbers in their simplest form, as follows:

- If you enter a number with fewer than 12 digits in a standard-width cell (which holds 8.43 characters), Excel adjusts the width of the column to accommodate the entry.

- If you enter a number with 12 or more digits, Excel displays it in scientific notation. For example, if you enter 12345678912345 in a standard-width cell, Excel displays 1.23457E+13 (1.23457 times 10 to the 13th power).

- If you enter a value with many decimal places, Excel might round it. For example, if you enter 123456.789 in a standard-width cell, Excel displays 123456.8.

- If you manually set the width of a column and then enter a numeric value that is too large to be displayed in its entirety, Excel displays pound signs (#) instead of the value.

➤ **To complete a data entry**

→ Click the **Enter** button (the check mark) on the formula bar to complete the entry and stay in the same cell.

→ Press **Enter** or the **Down Arrow** key to complete the entry and move down to the next cell in the same column.

→ Press the **Tab** key or the **Right Arrow** key to complete the entry and move (to the right) to the next cell in the same row, or to the next cell in the table (which might be the first cell of the next row).

→ Press **Shift+Enter** or the **Up Arrow** key to complete the entry and move up to the previous cell in the same column.

→ Press **Shift+Tab** or the **Left Arrow** key to complete the entry and move (to the left) to the previous cell in the same row.

1 Create and manage workbooks and worksheets

The skills tested in this section of the Microsoft Office Specialist exam for Microsoft Excel 2013 relate to creating and managing workbooks and worksheets. Specifically, the following objectives are associated with this set of skills:

1.1 Create workbooks and worksheets
1.2 Navigate through worksheets and workbooks
1.3 Format worksheets and workbooks
1.4 Customize options and views for worksheets and workbooks
1.5 Configure worksheets and workbooks to print or save

An Excel workbook contains one or more worksheets. The data on a worksheet can be related to data in other areas of the workbook or in other workbooks.

A single workbook can contain a vast amount of raw and calculated data. You can structure and format workbook content so that key information can be easily identified and so that data is presented correctly on the screen and when printed. You can locate information within a workbook by searching values, formula elements, or named objects.

There are many ways of optimizing the appearance and functionality of Excel for the processes you perform most frequently and to suit your individual preferences.

This chapter guides you in studying ways of creating, navigating through, formatting, printing, and saving the workbooks and worksheets in which you store information in Excel, and customizing elements of the Excel environment.

> **Practice Files** To complete the practice tasks in this chapter, you need the practice files contained in the MOSExcel2013\Objective1 practice file folder. For more information, see "Download the practice files" in this book's Introduction.

1.1 Create workbooks and worksheets

Creating new workbooks and worksheets

One of the ways in which Excel 2013 operates more efficiently than previous versions of Excel is by creating only necessary workbooks and worksheets. Instead of creating a workbook each time you start the program, Excel displays a start screen from which you can open an existing workbook or create a new workbook.

When Excel is running, you can create a blank or prepopulated workbook from the New page of the Backstage view.

By default, a new workbook includes only one worksheet. You can add blank worksheets to the workbook or copy or move worksheets from another workbook.

> **Tip** When you create Excel objects such as charts, PivotTables, and PivotCharts, you can insert them on the worksheet that contains the data or on sheets that are dedicated to the new object.

> ➤ **To create a blank workbook**

→ Start Excel. On the Start screen, press **Esc** or click **Blank Workbook**.

→ On the **New** page of the **Backstage** view, click **Blank Workbook**.

→ From the program window, press **Ctrl+N**.

> ➤ **To create a workbook from a template**

→ On the Start screen or on the **New** page of the **Backstage** view, do one of the following:

○ Click a featured template.

○ Enter a template type or subject in the **Search** box, and then press **Enter** or click the **Search** button. Click a template thumbnail to preview its contents and then create a workbook by clicking **Create** in the preview window; or double-click the template thumbnail to create a workbook without first previewing it.

○ Click the **Personal** heading, and then double-click a custom or downloaded workbook template.

> ➤ **To insert a new worksheet**

→ Click the **New sheet** button at the right end of the worksheet tab section.

→ On the **Home** tab, in the **Cells** group, click the **Insert** arrow, and then click **Insert Sheet**.

Or

1. Right-click the worksheet tab before which you want to insert a new worksheet, and then click **Insert**.

2. On the **General** page of the **Insert** dialog box, click **Worksheet**, and then click **OK**.

Reusing existing content

You can add a worksheet from another workbook by moving or copying it from the original (source) workbook.

If the content you want to use exists in another format, such as in a delimited text file, you can import the file contents into a worksheet in Excel. Alternatively, you can open the file in Excel and copy only the data you want from the file.

Import Data dialog box:

> **Import Data**   ?   ✕
>
> Select how you want to view this data in your workbook.
>
> ▦ ● Table
> ▧ ○ PivotTable Report
> ▨ ○ PivotChart
> ▦ ○ Power View Report
> ▤ ○ Only Create Connection
>
> Where do you want to put the data?
>
> ● Existing worksheet:
>
> [=$A$1   ] 🔳
>
> ○ New worksheet
>
> ☐ Add this data to the Data Model
>
> [Properties...]   [OK]   [Cancel]

> **Tip** Importing a file disconnects the contents from the source file, whereas opening the file permits you to edit the file contents in Excel.

➤ To move or copy a worksheet

→ On the tab bar, drag the worksheet tab to the new position to move it.

→ Press **Ctrl** and drag the worksheet tab to the new position to copy it.

Or

1. Right-click the worksheet tab, and then click **Move or Copy**.

   Or

   On the **Home** tab, in the **Cells** group, click **Format**, and then in the **Organize Sheets** section, click **Move or Copy Sheet**.

2. In the **Move or Copy** dialog box, do one of the following, and then click **OK**:

   ○ To move the worksheet within the same workbook, in the **Before sheet** box, click the worksheet before which you want to insert the worksheet.

   ○ To move the worksheet to another open workbook, click the destination workbook in the **To book** list. Then in the **Before sheet** box, click the worksheet before which you want to insert the worksheet.

   ○ To move the worksheet to a new workbook, click **(New book)** in the **To book** list.

   Or

In the **Move or Copy** dialog box, select the **Create a copy** check box, do one of the following, and then click **OK**:

- ○ To create a copy within the same workbook, in the **Before sheet** box, click the worksheet before which you want to insert the copy.

- ○ To create a copy in another open workbook, click the destination workbook in the **To book** list. Then in the **Before sheet** box, click the worksheet before which you want to insert the copy.

- ○ To create a copy in a new workbook, click (**New book**) in the **To book** list.

> **Tip** You can move or copy a worksheet to an existing workbook only if that workbook is open.

➤ **To import the contents of a text file**

1. On the **Data** tab, in the **Get External Data** group, click **From Text**.

2. In the **Import Text File** dialog box, browse to and select the text file you want to import, and then click **Import**.

3. On the **Step 1** page of the **Text Import Wizard**, click **Delimited** or **Fixed width** to indicate the way that data in the text file is separated. Specify the first row of data you want to import (this will almost always be 1), and select the **My data has headers** check box if applicable. Then click **Next**.

> **Tip** The preview at the bottom of the page displays the data being imported.

4. On the **Step 2** page of the **Text Import Wizard**, select the character or characters that separate the field content within the text file, and then click **Next**.

5. On the **Step 3** page of the **Text Import Wizard**, do the following, and then click **Finish**:

- ○ For each column of numeric data in the preview that requires specific number formatting, click the column and then specify the number format.

- ○ For each column you want to exclude from the import operation, click the column and then click **Do not import column (skip)**.

6. In the **Import Data** dialog box, click the location to which you want to import the data, and then click **OK**.

➤ **To open a non-native file in Excel**

1. On the **Open** page of the **Backstage** view, select the storage location from which you want to open the file, and then click **Browse**.

2. In the **Open** dialog box, in the list of file types, click **All Files (*.*)** or click the specific type of file you want to open.

3. Browse to and select the file you want to open, and then click **Open**.

Practice tasks

The practice file for these tasks is located in the MOSExcel2013\Objective1 practice file folder. Save the results of the tasks in the same folder.

- Create a workbook based on a sales report template of your choice, and save it as *Sales Data*. Leave the workbook open.

- Open the *Excel_1-1* workbook, and complete the following tasks:
  - Move the Source Data worksheet so it is the last worksheet in the workbook.
  - Make a copy of the Source Data worksheet as the last worksheet in the Sales Data workbook.

1.2 Navigate through worksheets and workbooks

Locating data and worksheet elements

You can easily locate specific values, formula content, comment text, and formatting anywhere within a workbook. Using the Find operation, you can search the entire workbook or a specific worksheet for text and formatting in formulas, calculated values, or comments.

Find and Replace

Find | Replace

Find what: | 2011 | | No Format Set | Format... ▾

Within: Workbook ☐ Match case
Search: By Rows ☐ Match entire cell contents
Look in: Formulas

Options <<

Find All | Find Next | Close

If you're looking for a specific element or type of element, you can locate it by using the Go To and Go To Special commands. From the Go To dialog box, you can locate any named element (such as a cell, cell range, named range, table, or chart). From the Go To Special dialog box, you can locate comments, formulas or specific formula elements, blank cells, objects, row or column differences, precedents and dependents, conditional formatting, data validation, and more.

Go To

Go to:
$C$10
$E$3:$E$8
$A$1
Table1
Table13

Reference:
C10

Special... | OK

Go To Special

Select
○ Comments
○ Constants
○ Formulas
  ☑ Numbers
  ☑ Text
  ☑ Logicals
  ☑ Errors
○ Blanks
○ Current region
○ Current array
○ Objects

○ Row differences
○ Column differences
◉ Precedents
○ Dependents
  ◉ Direct only
  ○ All levels
○ Last cell
○ Visible cells only
○ Conditional formats
○ Data validation
  ◉ All
  ○ Same

OK | Cancel

➤ **To search for text**

1. On the **Home** tab, in the **Editing** group, display the **Find & Select** list, and then click **Find** (or press **Ctrl+F**).

2. On the **Find** page of the **Find and Replace** dialog box, enter the text you want to locate, and if necessary, click **Options** to display the search parameters.

3. Specify the following search parameters:

   ○ In the **Within** list, click **Sheet** or **Workbook**.

   ○ In the **Search** list, click **By Rows** or **By Columns**.

   ○ In the **Look in** list, click **Formulas**, **Values**, or **Comments**.

4. Select the **Match case** or **Match entire cell contents** check boxes to further restrict your search.

5. Click **Find Next**.

➤ **To search for formatting**

1. On the **Find** page of the **Find and Replace** dialog box, click the **Format** button.

2. In the **Find Format** dialog box, specify the number, alignment, font, border, fill, or protection formatting you want to find. Then click **OK**.

3. In the **Find and Replace** dialog box, click **Find Next**.

➤ **To search for matching formatting**

1. On the **Find** page of the **Find and Replace** dialog box, click the **Format** arrow, and then click **Choose Format From Cell**.

2. When the pointer changes to an eyedropper, select the cell on which you want to base your search.

3. In the **Find and Replace** dialog box, click **Find Next**.

➤ **To move to a named cell, range, or workbook element**

→ On the formula bar, click the **Name** box arrow, and then select the named element.

Or

1. In the **Find & Select** list, click **Go To** (or press **Ctrl+G**).

2. In the **Go To** dialog box, click a named element in the **Go to** list, and then click **OK**.

➤ **To move to a location that has a specific property**

1. In the **Find & Select** list, click **Go To Special** (or click **Special** in the **Go To** dialog box).

2. In the **Go To Special** dialog box, click the property for which you want to search, and then click **OK**.

Inserting hyperlinks

Excel worksheets can include hyperlinks that provide a quick way to connect to related information or to create a pre-addressed email message. You can create a hyperlink from any cell content to any of the hyperlink locations supported by the Office 2013 programs—another location on the worksheet, in the workbook, in an external document, or on the web.

By default, hyperlinks are formatted as underlined, colored text. (The active and followed hyperlink colors are specified by the theme.) Clicking the hyperlink text in the cell that contains the hyperlink displays the hyperlink target.

> **Tip** To select a cell that contains a hyperlink, click part of the cell away from the hyperlink or click and hold down the mouse button until the pointer changes to a plus sign.

➤ **To create a hyperlink to a webpage**

→ Enter a URL in the cell, and then press **Enter**.

Or

1. Select the cell or element from which you want to link.

2. On the **Insert** tab, in the **Links** group, click the **Hyperlink** button (or press **Ctrl+K**).

3. In the **Insert Hyperlink** dialog box, in the **Link to** list, click **Existing File or Web Page**.

4. In the **Address** box, enter the URL of the webpage you want to link to.

Or

Click the **Browse the Web** button (the button labeled with a globe and magnifying glass). In the web browser window that opens (not a previously open window), display the webpage you want to link to, and click the **Insert Hyperlink** dialog box to copy the webpage address from the browser address bar to the **Address** box of the dialog box. Then minimize or close the browser window.

> **Tip** If the webpage address doesn't copy to the Address box in a valid format—for example if the webpage is on a Microsoft SharePoint site—manually copy the address from the browser address bar to the Address box of the Insert Hyperlink dialog box.

5. If you want to display text other than the target when a user points to the hyperlink, click the **ScreenTip** button, enter the ScreenTip text, and then click **OK**.

> **Tip** When inserting a hyperlink from a cell that contains text (not numeric data), the Text To Display box is active. You can change the text in the cell by entering alternative text in the Text To Display box.

6. In the **Insert Hyperlink** dialog box, click **OK**.

➤ **To create a hyperlink to an existing file**

1. Select the cell or element from which you want to link. Then click the **Hyperlink** button (or press **Ctrl+K**).

2. In the **Insert Hyperlink** dialog box, in the **Link to** list, click **Existing File or Web Page**.

3. In the **Look in** area, browse to the file you want to link to.

4. In the **Insert Hyperlink** dialog box, click **OK**.

➤ **To create an Excel workbook and a hyperlink to it**

1. Select the cell or element from which you want to link. Then click the **Hyperlink** button (or press **Ctrl+K**).

2. In the **Insert Hyperlink** dialog box, in the **Link to** list, click **Create New Document**.

3. In the **Name of new document** box, enter a name for the workbook.

> **Tip** Do not enter the file extension. The Create New Document hyperlink in an Excel workbook automatically creates an Excel workbook.

4. To create the document in a folder other than your Documents folder, click the **Change** button. Then, in the **Create New Document** dialog box, browse to the folder in which you want to save the file, and click **OK**.

5. In the **When to edit** area, do one of the following:

   ○ Click **Edit the new document later** to create a blank workbook.

   ○ Click **Edit the new document now** to create a workbook and open it in Excel.

6. In the **Insert Hyperlink** dialog box, click **OK**.

➤ **To create a hyperlink to a worksheet or named range within the workbook**

1. Select the cell or element from which you want to link. Then click the **Hyperlink** button (or press **Ctrl+K**).

2. In the **Insert Hyperlink** dialog box, in the **Link to** list, click **Place in This Document**.

3. In the **Or select a place in this document** box, click the heading or bookmark you want to link to.

4. In the **Insert Hyperlink** dialog box, click **OK**.

➤ **To create a hyperlink that creates a pre-addressed email message**

1. Select the cell or element from which you want to link. Then click the **Hyperlink** button (or press **Ctrl+K**).

2. In the **Insert Hyperlink** dialog box, in the **Link to** list, click **E-mail Address**.

3. In the **E-mail address** box, enter the email address of the message recipient.

4. In the **Subject** box, enter the message subject.

5. In the **Insert Hyperlink** dialog box, click **OK**.

Practice tasks

The practice files for these tasks are located in the MOSExcel2013\Objective1 practice file folder. Save the results of the tasks in the same folder.

- Open the *Excel_1-2a* workbook, and complete the following tasks on the Product List worksheet by using the techniques described in this section:

  - Move to the first cell that contains a comment.

  - Move to the cell range named Berry_bushes.

  - Move to cell F13.

  - Create a hyperlink from cell F13 to the cell range named Berry_bushes.

  - Move to the cell at the intersection of the last active row and column in the worksheet.

- Open the *Excel_1-2b* workbook, and complete the following tasks on the Employees worksheet:

  - In cell C12, enter a hyperlink to the website located at *www.adventure-works.com*.

  - Edit the hyperlink so that the cell displays *Please visit our website* instead of the URL.

1.3 Format worksheets and workbooks

Modifying page setup

You can control the basic footprint of printed worksheets by defining the paper size and orientation, changing the page margins, and changing the space allocated to the header and footer. By configuring these page setup options, you define the space that is available for the content on an individual page when it is printed or displayed in Print Layout view.

Tip If your content doesn't fit within the allocated area, you can adjust the way it fits on the page by scaling it, either from the Page Setup tab or from the Print page. For more information, see section 1.5, "Configuring worksheets and workbooks to print or save."

➤ To change the page margins

1. On the **Page Layout** tab, in the **Page Setup** group, click the **Margins** button.

2. On the **Margins** menu, do one of the following:

   ○ Click the standard margin setting you want.

   ○ Click the **Custom Margins** command. Then on the **Margins** page of the **Page Setup** dialog box, specify the **Top**, **Bottom**, **Left**, and **Right** margins, and click **OK**.

➤ To change the page orientation

→ On the **Page Layout** tab, in the **Page Setup** group, click the **Orientation** button, and then click **Portrait** or **Landscape**.

➤ To set a standard paper size

→ On the **Page Layout** tab, in the **Page Setup** group, click the **Size** button, and then click the paper size you want.

➤ To set a custom paper size

1. On the **Page Layout** tab, in the **Page Setup** group, click the **Size** button, and then click **More Paper Sizes**.

2. On the **Page** page of the **Page Setup** dialog box, click **Options**.

3. On the **Paper/Quality** page of the **Printer Properties** dialog box, in the **Paper Options** area, click **Custom**.

4. In the **Custom Paper Size** dialog box, enter a name for the custom size, enter the width and length of the paper, specify the units of measurement, click **Save**, and then click **Close**.

5. Click **OK** in each of the open dialog boxes.

> **Tip** The available print settings depend on the currently selected printer.

Inserting page elements

You can display information on every page of a printed worksheet, and also in Page Layout view, by inserting it in the page headers and footers. You can have a different header and footer on the first page or different headers and footers on odd and even pages. When you create a header or footer, Excel displays the workbook in a view that is similar to Page Layout view, and the Design tool tab appears on the ribbon.

An active header or footer is divided into three sections in which you can enter information either manually or from the Design tool tab. (The commands on the Insert tab are not available while the header or footer is active for editing.)

You can enter document information and properties such as the current or total page number, current date or time, file path, file name, or sheet name from the Design tool tab, or you can enter and format text the same way you would in the worksheet body. You can also insert an image, such as a company logo.

If you want to display and print an image or text on a worksheet, for example to denote draft or confidential information or to indicate copyright ownership, you can simulate a watermark in the following ways:

- **Insert a graphic in the header or footer.** The advantages of this method are that the graphic appears on all printed pages, and you can easily apply a "wash out" effect so that it looks like a true watermark. A possible disadvantage is that the graphic is anchored in the header or footer rather than centered on the page.

> **Important** If you anchor the graphic in the footer, you must include some content in the header, or the graphic will not be visible in the content area.

- **Insert a background image on the worksheet.** The advantage of this method is that the image appears on all printed pages. The disadvantage is that Excel tiles background images, so you must either choose a page-sized image or an image that repeats gracefully. You must also manually apply any washout effects before selecting the image.

- **Insert a WordArt object on the worksheet.** The advantages of this method are that it provides a simple way of creating and formatting text that is appropriate for a watermark, you can position it anywhere on the page, and you can rotate the WordArt object however you want. A possible disadvantage is that you must place the WordArt object on each page on which you want it to appear.

Graphic watermark in header   WordArt watermark

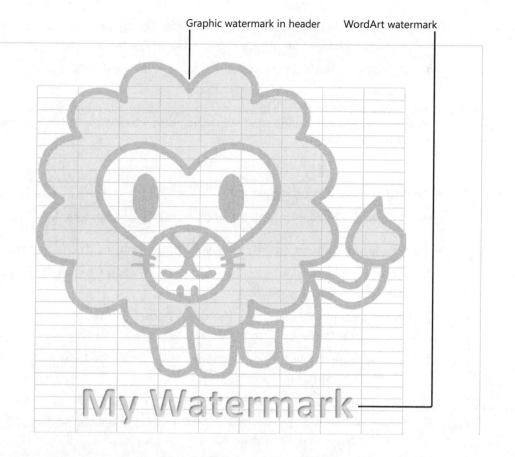

➤ **To insert content in the page header and footer**

1. On the **Insert** tab, in the **Text** group, click **Header & Footer**, or in **Page Layout** view, click **Click to add header**.

2. Click the left, center, or right header section. Then do any of the following:

   ○ To insert a document property in the active header section, select document information from the **Header** list in the **Header & Footer** group on the **Design** tool tab, or click a button in the **Header & Footer Elements** group.

   ○ in the **Header & Footer Elements** group, click **Picture**, and then browse to the local or online picture you want to display in the active header section.

   ○ Manually enter information in the active header section.

3. To display different headers on the first and following pages, or on odd and even pages, select the corresponding check box in the **Options** group, and then insert the header information you want for each set of pages.

4. To move to the footer, click **Click to add footer** on any page, or on the **Design** tool tab, in the **Navigation** group, click the **Go to Footer** button.

5. To close the header and footer areas, click in the workbook body.

> **Tip** If you decide to insert a header or footer just before printing, you can do so from the Header/Footer page of the Page Setup dialog box, which is accessible from the Print page of the Backstage view.

➤ **To edit the header or footer**

➜ Activate the header or footer, and then make your changes.

➤ **To simulate a picture watermark by adding a picture to the header or footer**

1. Activate the header or footer and click the left, center, or right section in which you want to anchor the watermark.

2. On the **Design** tool tab, in the **Header & Footer Elements** group, click **Picture**, and then browse to the local or online picture you want to display as a watermark.

3. With **&[Picture]** selected in the header or footer, in the **Header & Footer Elements** group, click **Format Picture**.

4. On the **Size** page of the **Format Picture** dialog box, set the height and width of the picture so that it is approximately the size of the page (or the size you want it to extend from the anchor location).

5. On the **Picture** page of the **Format Picture** dialog box, in the **Image control** area, click **Washout** in the **Color** list. Make any other color adjustments you want, and then click **OK**.

➤ **To simulate a picture watermark by adding a background picture**

1. On the **Page Layout** tab, in the **Page Setup** group, click the **Background** button.

2. From the **Insert Picture** dialog box, locate and insert the picture file you want to use as the background. (Use standard techniques to locate a file on your computer or online.)

➤ **To simulate a text watermark**

1. On the **Insert** tab, in the **Text** group, click the **WordArt** button.

2. In the **WordArt** gallery, click a transparent text style.

3. Enter the text of the watermark.

4. Adjust the rotation, size, and location of the WordArt object as necessary.

Changing workbook themes and colors

You can enhance the look of an entire workbook by applying a predefined theme—a combination of colors, fonts, and effects. In the Themes gallery, you can point to a theme to display a live preview of its effect on the workbook elements before you apply it.

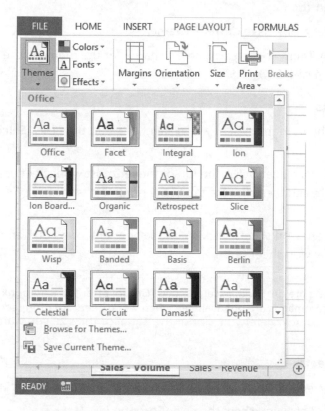

If you like certain aspects of different themes (for example, the colors of one theme and the fonts of another), you can mix and match theme elements. If you create a combination of theme elements that you would like to use with other worksheets, you can save the combination as a new theme. After you save a theme in the default Document Themes folder, the theme is available in the Custom section of the Themes gallery.

To apply formatting to several worksheets at once, group the worksheets, and then perform the formatting operation.

➤ **To apply a theme to a worksheet**

1. On the **Page Layout** tab, in the **Themes** group, click the **Themes** button.

2. In the **Themes** gallery, click the theme you want.

➤ **To modify a theme**

1. In the **Themes** group, click the **Colors**, **Fonts**, or **Effects** button.

2. In the gallery, click the theme element you want.

➤ **To save a customized theme**

1. In the **Themes** gallery, click **Save Current Theme**.

2. In the **Save Current Theme** dialog box, enter a name for the theme in the **File name** box, and then click **Save**.

➤ **To group worksheets**

→ To group all worksheets, right-click any worksheet tab, and then click **Select All Sheets**.

→ To group adjacent worksheets, click the tab of the leftmost worksheet you want to group, press **Shift**, and then click the tab of the rightmost worksheet you want to group.

→ To group nonadjacent worksheets, click any worksheet tab, press **Ctrl**, and then click each additional worksheet tab.

> **Tip** When worksheets are grouped, Excel displays [Group] after the workbook name in the title bar. Many commands are not available when worksheets are grouped.

➤ **To ungroup worksheets**

→ Click the tab of any worksheet.

→ Right-click the tab of any worksheet that is not grouped.

→ Right-click the tab of any grouped worksheet, and then click **Ungroup Sheets**.

> **Tip** When a workbook contains several worksheets, it can be helpful to assign different colors to the tabs to categorize them or to make them easily distinguishable. To change the color of a worksheet tab, right-click the tab, click Tab Color, and then click the color you want.

Modifying rows and columns

Inserting and deleting rows and columns is a natural part of worksheet development, and in Excel 2013, it couldn't be easier. You can insert an entire row above the selected cell or an entire column to the left of it. If you want to insert a cell instead of a row or column, you are given the option of making room by moving cells down or to the right.

Similarly, you can delete a selected row or column, or you can delete only the selected cells, optionally specifying how the remaining cells should fill the space.

In addition to inserting empty rows, columns, or cells, you can insert cut or copied cell contents directly into an existing table or data range with one command. When you insert a range of cells rather than an entire row or column, Excel requests instructions for making room before inserting a similarly shaped range.

> **Tip** Always select a single cell when inserting cut or copied cells. If you select a range that is a different size and shape from the one you want to insert, you will get an error message.

By default, worksheet rows have a standard height of 15 points, or 0.21 inches, and their height increases and decreases to accommodate the number of lines in their longest entry. You can manually change the height of a row, but it is best to leave the row height dynamic to accommodate future changes, unless you have a good reason to specify a height. For example, you might want to specify a narrow row to create a visual break between blocks of data. (You can restore dynamic height adjustment if you need to.)

Worksheet columns have a standard width of 8.43 characters (in the default font), or 0.72 inches, and their width is not dynamic. You are more likely to want to change column width than row height, usually to accommodate long cell entries. You can have Excel adjust a column to fit its longest entry, or you can adjust it manually to up to 255 characters. In conjunction with text wrapping, adjusting column widths is a key technique for making as much data as possible visible on the screen or page.

> **Tip** When the ruler is hidden, row heights are specified in points and column widths in characters. When the ruler is displayed, row heights and column widths are specified in inches.

For the purposes of height and width adjustments, selecting a single cell in a row or column is the same as selecting the entire row or column. You can change the height or width of multiple rows or columns at the same time by selecting them and then performing the resizing operation.

➤ To insert rows or columns

1. Select the number of rows you want to insert, starting with the row above which you want the inserted rows to appear, or select the number of columns you want to insert, starting with the column to the left of which you want the inserted columns to appear.

2. On the **Home** tab, in the **Cells** group, click the **Insert** button.

Or

Right-click the selection, and then click **Insert**.

➤ To delete selected rows or columns

→ On the **Home** tab, in the **Cells** group, click the **Delete** button.

➤ To change the height of a selected row

→ Drag the bottom border of the row selector up or down.

> **Tip** As you drag the border, a ScreenTip displays the current row height in either points or inches and in pixels.

Or

1. On the **Home** tab, in the **Cells** group, display the **Format** list, and then click **Row Height**.

2. In the **Row Height** dialog box, specify the height you want, and then click **OK**.

➤ To change the width of a selected column

→ Drag the right border of the column selector to the left or right.

> **Tip** As you drag the border, a ScreenTip displays the current column width in either characters or inches and in pixels.

Or

1. On the **Home** tab, in the **Cells** group, display the **Format** list, and then click **Column Width**.

2. In the **Column Width** dialog box, specify the width you want, and then click **OK**.

➤ **To size a column or row to fit its contents**

→ Double-click the right border of the column heading or the bottom border of the row heading.

→ On the **Home** tab, in the **Cells** group, display the **Format** list, and then click **AutoFit Column Width**.

→ On the **Home** tab, in the **Cells** group, display the **Format** list, and then click **AutoFit Row Height**.

> **Tip** You can adjust the width of all the columns in a worksheet at the same time. Click the worksheet selector to select the entire worksheet, and then double-click the border between any two columns. Every populated column resizes to fit its contents. Empty columns remain unchanged.

Configuring data validation

A simple way to ensure that worksheets produce the expected results is to take measures to ensure that the data being entered meets necessary criteria. This is especially important in workbooks that you will be distributing for other people to populate with data. You can do this in two ways:

- By limiting entries to those the user chooses from a list that you provide.

- By checking the data against specific criteria as it is entered. This is referred to as *validating the data*.

You can validate data in several ways. For any numeric, date, or time validation check, you can specify whether you want to allow the entry to be between two values, not between two values, greater than, less than, equal to, or not equal to a value. Each of the values to be used for validation can be a specific value, a reference to a cell on the worksheet or a cell on another worksheet, or calculated with a formula referencing cells. With this, very complex validation rules can be created. For example, you could create a rule in a budget worksheet specifying that the budget item for charitable contributions should be at least as large as the previous year, but no more than 10 percent of the net pretax profit.

You can restrict cell content to the following data types:

- **Any value** This is the default value.

- **Whole number** An integer, either positive or negative.

- **Decimal** Any type of number, whole or otherwise, positive or negative.

- **List** An input list from which the user can select only a specific value.

- **Date** Any recognized date format. You can specify an allowable range of dates.

- **Time** Any recognized time format. You can specify an allowable range of times.

- **Text length** A maximum number of characters.

- **Custom** Any valid Excel formula that equates to True or False. To validate the value that is being entered, reference the cell in the formula. For example, to check whether the value in C3 contains text, use the formula =*ISTEXT(C3)*.

When the data entered in a cell doesn't meet the data validation criteria, Excel displays an error message. You can also have Excel display instructions to guide the user in inserting the correct type of data in the cell. The input message resembles a comment, and is visible only when the cell is active.

➤ **To restrict entries to a specific list of options**

1. On the worksheet on which you will create the input list, enter the items you want to make available from the list into a range of cells. Choose a location that will not interfere with data entry.

   Or

   On a worksheet other than the one on which you will create the input list, enter the list items in a range of cells.

2. Select the cell or range of cells for which you want to create the input list.

3. On the **Data** tab, in the **Data Tools** group, click the **Data Validation** button.

4. On the **Settings** tab of the **Data Validation** dialog box, in the **Allow** list, click **List**.

5. Position the cursor in the **Source** box, then select or enter the cell range containing the list items you created in step 1.

6. In the **Data Validation** dialog box, click **OK**.

➤ **To restrict entries to those meeting specific criteria**

1. Select the cell or range of cells for which you want to enforce data validation criteria.

2. On the **Data** tab, in the **Data Tools** group, click the **Data Validation** button.

3. On the **Settings** tab of the **Data Validation** dialog box, click the **Allow** arrow, and then in the list, click the type of data you want to allow.

4. In the data type–specific criteria boxes that appear, select or enter the criteria that data in the selected cells must meet. Then click **OK**.

> **Tip** Take care when setting up data validation checks that you don't inadvertently disallow valid data. Test your data validation criteria by entering both valid and invalid data and verifying that you get the expected results.

➤ **To configure an input message to support data validation**

1. On the **Input Message** page of the **Data Validation** dialog box, select the **Show input message when cell is selected** check box.

2. In the **Title** box, enter the text you want to appear in bold font at the beginning of the input message.

3. In the **Input message** box, enter the text you want to appear in regular font after the input message title.

4. Click **OK**.

➤ **To modify the standard error message**

1. On the **Error Alert** page of the **Data Validation** dialog box, select the **Show error alert after invalid data is entered** check box.

2. In the **Style** list, click the type of icon you want to display in the error message: **Stop** to display a white X in a red circle, **Warning** to display a black exclamation point in a yellow triangle, or **Information** to display a white lowercase letter *i* in a blue circle.

3. In the **Title** box, enter the text you want to appear in the title bar of the error message dialog box.

4. In the **Error message** box, enter the text you want to appear in the body of the error message dialog box.

5. Click **OK**.

➤ **To locate worksheet cells that have data validation configured**

→ On the **Home** tab, in the **Editing** group, click **Find & Select**, and then in the list, click **Data Validation**.

➤ **To cancel data validation**

1. Select one or more cells from which you want to remove data validation.

2. To cancel all instances of the selected data validation criteria in the worksheet, select the **Apply these changes to all other cells with the same settings** check box on the **Settings** page of the **Data Validation** dialog box.

3. On any page of the dialog box, click **Clear All**, and then click **OK**.

Practice tasks

The practice files for these tasks are located in the MOSExcel2013\Objective1 practice file folder. Save the results of the tasks in the same folder.

- Open the *Excel_1-3a* workbook, and complete the following tasks:
    - Change each of the visible worksheet tabs to a different color.
    - Configure the JanFeb worksheet to print horizontally on two pages of letter-size paper.
    - Configure the MarApr worksheet to print on two pages of A5-size paper.
    - Configure the MayJun worksheet to print at 50 percent of its actual size.
- Open the *Excel_1-3b* workbook, and complete the following tasks on the Orders worksheet:
    - Create a header that will print on all the pages of the worksheet except the first page. On the left side of the header, enter today's date; in the center section, enter the name of the workbook; and on the right side, enter the page number.
    - In Normal view, change the center section of the header to reflect the name of the worksheet instead of the workbook.
    - Remove the page numbers from the header, and then add page numbers that print at the bottom of each page.
- In the *Excel_1-3c* workbook, on the Order Details worksheet, add a data validation check to the Discount column to ensure that the value is between 0 and .2 (in other words, that the discount does not exceed 20 percent). Include an input message and display a warning if an incorrect value is entered.
- In the *Excel_1-3d* workbook, display the By Product-Customer worksheet and ensure that at least one outline section is expanded. Then group all the worksheets and apply the Austin theme to the worksheet group.

1.4 Customize options and views for worksheets and workbooks

Displaying different views of worksheets

From the View toolbar at the bottom of the program window, or from the View tab, you can switch among three views of a worksheet:

- **Normal** The worksheet is displayed in the window at 100 percent magnification or at whatever zoom level you select. Page breaks are indicated by black dashed lines.

- **Page Layout** Each worksheet page appears as it will when printed, with space between the individual pages. A ruler appears at the left edge of the window next to the optional row headings. The page header and footer are visible and you can select them for editing.

- **Page Break Preview** The entire worksheet is displayed in the window, with page breaks indicated by bold blue dashed lines and page numbers displayed in the center of each page. You can change the page breaks by dragging the blue lines.

To maximize your work area, you can display a worksheet in full-screen mode, so that only the title bar is visible. To increase the vertical space of the work area but still have easy access to commands, you can hide the ribbon so that only its tabs are visible, and hide the formula bar.

The View Shortcuts toolbar includes buttons for changing the view of the document window.

View Shortcuts toolbar

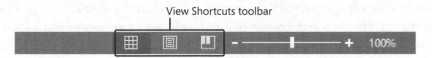

From the Zoom toolbar at the bottom of the program window, or from the Zoom group on the View tab, you can change the zoom level of a worksheet in any range from 10 percent to 400 percent. You can zoom the entire worksheet or select a range of cells and have Excel determine the zoom level necessary to fit the selection in the window.

➤ **To display a standard worksheet view**

→ On the **View Shortcuts** toolbar near the right end of the status bar, click the **Normal**, **Page Layout**, or **Page Break Preview** button.

→ On the **View** tab, in the **Workbook Views** group, click the **Normal**, **Page Layout**, or **Page Break Preview** button.

➤ **To zoom in or out in 10-percent increments**

→ On the status bar, click the **Zoom In (+)** or **Zoom Out (-)** button.

➤ **To change the zoom level dynamically**

→ Drag the **Zoom** slider to the left to zoom out or to the right to zoom in.

➤ **To zoom to a specific magnification**

1. On the **View** tab, in the **Zoom** group, click the **Zoom** button.

   Or

   On the status bar, click the **Zoom level** button.

2. In the **Zoom** dialog box, click a specific magnification level, or click **Custom** and then enter a value from 10 to 400. Then click **OK**.

➤ **To zoom in on selected cells**

1. Select the cell or cell range you want to zoom in on.

2. Open the **Zoom** dialog box, click **Fit selection**, and then click **OK**.

Displaying multiple parts of a workbook

It can be cumbersome to work in a worksheet that is too long or wide to display legibly in the program window, to scroll up and down or back and forth to view data elsewhere in the worksheet, or to switch back and forth between multiple worksheets in the same workbook if you frequently need to access information in both of them.

You can view multiple parts of a worksheet at one time by freezing rows or columns so they stay in view while you scroll the rest of the worksheet, by splitting the window so you can independently scroll and work in two or four views of the worksheet within the same program window, or by displaying multiple instances of the workbook in separate program windows. Regardless of the technique you use, changes you make to the workbook content in any one view are immediately reflected in the others.

> **Tip** Another way to display disparate rows or columns together on one screen is to hide the rows or columns between them.

Multiple instances of a workbook

➤ To freeze the first row or column of a worksheet

→ On the **View** tab, in the **Window** group, click the **Freeze Panes** button, and then click **Freeze Top Row** or **Freeze First Column**.

➤ To freeze multiple rows or columns

1. Select the row below or column to the right of those you want to freeze, by clicking the row selector or column selector.

2. On the **View** tab, in the **Window** group, click the **Freeze Panes** button, and then click **Freeze Panes**.

➤ To simultaneously freeze columns and rows

1. Select the cell that is below and to the right of the intersection of the row and column you want to freeze.

2. On the **View** tab, in the **Window** group, click the **Freeze Panes** button, and then click **Freeze Panes**.

> **Tip** You can freeze as many columns and rows as you like depending on what cell is selected when you invoke the Freeze Panes command. Selecting a cell in row 1 freezes the columns to the left of that cell. Selecting a cell in column A freezes the rows above that cell. Selecting cell A1 freezes the panes at the midpoint of the current window (the top half of the rows and the left half of the columns). Selecting a cell other than those in row 1 and column A freezes the rows above and columns to the left of the cell.

➤ **To unfreeze all rows and columns**

→ On the **View** tab, in the **Window** group, click the **Freeze Panes** button, and then click **Unfreeze Panes**.

➤ **To display multiple views of a workbook in the same program window**

1. To split the window into two parts, click a cell in row 1 or column A.

Or

To split the window into four parts, click the cell above and to the left of where you want to split the panes.

2. On the **View** tab, in the **Window** group, click **Split**.

➤ **To modify the split between windows**

→ Drag the vertical or horizontal split bar to the row or column where you want to split the window.

➤ **To remove a split from a program window**

→ Double-click the split bar that divides the pane.

→ Drag the vertical split bar to the top of the scroll bar.

→ Drag the horizontal split bar to the right end of the scroll bar.

➤ **To display multiple views of a workbook in separate program windows**

1. On the **View** tab, in the **Window** group, click the **New Window** button to open another instance of the workbook.

> **Tip** You can open several instances of the workbook; Excel displays the instance number after the workbook name in the program window title bar.

2. Arrange the workbook windows as you want, or click the **Arrange All** button and then in the **Arrange Windows** dialog box, click **Tiled**, **Horizontal**, **Vertical**, or **Cascade**. To arrange only the instances of the active workbook, select the **Windows of active workbook** check box. Then click **OK**.

3. Display the worksheet, worksheet section, or workbook element you want in each workbook window.

4. To return to a single program window, close the others. It is not necessary to save changes in any but the last open instance of the workbook.

Hiding and displaying workbook content

A workbook, particularly one that contains data calculations, PivotTables, or PivotCharts, might contain reference data that isn't otherwise required. You can hide rows, columns, or entire worksheets of data you don't need to use or don't want other people to see.

When you hide rows or columns, anyone who notices that column letters or row numbers are missing can unhide the information unless you protect the workbook. If you don't want to go to the trouble of enforcing protection, you can hide the row and column headings so that the hidden information is not as obvious. This leaves only a small gap in place of any hidden rows or columns. To entirely mask the rows and columns, you can also hide the gridlines.

Hidden columns D and E

	A	B	C	F	G	H
4	Days with AQI data	Days AQI was Good	Days AQI was Moderate	Maximum AQI value	90th percentile AQI value	Median AQI value
5	365	93	150	237	147	82
6	323	98	163	166	122	72
7	365	168	152	182	106	54
8	345	182	116	173	114	49
9	365	181	123	161	112	51
10	365	287	65	152	69	35
11	365	284	73	155	68	34
12	365	187	140	195	101	49

> **Tip** Many worksheets contain formulas for the purpose of calculating data. A formula is visible in the formula bar when you click the cell that contains it, but its resulting value is visible in the cell. You can display formulas in the worksheet by clicking the Show Formulas button in the Formula Auditing group on the Formulas tab, or by pressing Ctrl+'.

➤ **To hide a worksheet**

→ Right-click the worksheet tab, and then click **Hide**.

➤ **To display a hidden worksheet**

1. Right-click the worksheet tab, and then click **Unhide**.

2. In the **Unhide** dialog box, select the worksheet you want to display, and then click **OK**.

➤ **To hide selected rows or columns**

→ Right-click the selection, and then click **Hide**.

Or

1. On the **Home** tab, in the **Cells** group, display the **Format** list.

2. In the **Visibility** section of the **Format** list, point to **Hide & Unhide**, and then click **Hide Rows** to hide the selected row(s) or **Hide Columns** to hide the selected column(s).

➤ **To hide row and column headings**

→ On the **View** tab, in the **Show** group, clear the **Headings** check box.

➤ **To hide gridlines**

→ On the **View** tab, in the **Show** group, clear the **Gridlines** check box.

➤ **To unhide rows or columns**

1. Select the columns or rows on both sides of the hidden column(s) or row(s).

2. Right-click the selection, and then click **Unhide**.

Or

1. Select the rows or columns on both sides of the hidden rows or columns.

2. On the **Home** tab, in the **Cells** group, display the **Format** list.

3. In the **Visibility** section of the **Format** list, point to **Hide & Unhide**, and then click **Unhide Rows** to display the selected row(s) or **Unhide Columns** to display the selected column(s).

➤ **To unhide the first row or column of a worksheet**

1. In the **Name** box to the left of the formula bar, enter **A1**, and then press **Enter**.

2. On the **Home** tab, in the **Cells** group, display the **Format** list.

3. In the **Visibility** section of the **Format** list, point to **Hide & Unhide**, and then click **Unhide Rows** to display row 1, or **Unhide Columns** to display column A.

> **Tip** To find hidden cells in a worksheet, click the Find & Select button, click Go To Special, select Visible Cells Only, and then click OK. Cells adjacent to hidden cells are identified by a white border.

Customizing the Quick Access Toolbar

By default, buttons representing the Save, Undo, and Redo commands (and the Touch/ Mouse Mode command, when you're working on a touchscreen device) appear on the Quick Access Toolbar in the Excel program window. If you regularly use a few commands that are scattered on various tabs of the ribbon and you don't want to switch between tabs to access the commands, you can add them to the Quick Access Toolbar so that they're always available to you. You can add commands to the Quick Access Toolbar from the Customize Quick Access Toolbar menu (which includes 8 additional common commands), from the ribbon, or from the Excel Options dialog box. You can add any type of command to the Quick Access Toolbar, even a drop-down list of options or gallery of thumbnails.

You save time by placing frequently used commands on the Quick Access Toolbar. To save even more time, you can move the Quick Access Toolbar from its default position above the ribbon to below the ribbon, so your mouse has less distance to travel from the content you're working with to the command you want to invoke. If you add all the buttons you use most often to the Quick Access Toolbar, you can hide the ribbon to gain screen space.

You can modify the Quick Access Toolbar by adding, moving, separating, or removing commands. You can add commands in several ways, but you can modify and separate commands only from the Excel Options dialog box. From that dialog box, you can modify the Quick Access Toolbar that appears in the program window or create a custom Quick Access Toolbar that appears only in the currently active workbook.

➤ **To add commands to the Quick Access Toolbar**

➜ At the right end of the **Quick Access Toolbar**, click the **Customize Quick Access Toolbar** button (the arrow), and then click one of the common commands displayed on the menu.

➜ Right-click a command on the ribbon, and then click **Add to Quick Access Toolbar**.

Or

1. Display the **Quick Access Toolbar** page of the **Excel Options** dialog box.

2. In the **Choose commands from** list, click the group of commands from which you want to select.

3. In the **Choose commands** pane, locate the command you want to add. Then click the **Add** button.

> ➤ **To remove a command from the Quick Access Toolbar**

→ Right-click the command on the **Quick Access Toolbar**, and then click **Remove from Quick Access Toolbar**.

→ On the **Customize Quick Access Toolbar** menu, click any active command (indicated by a check mark) to remove it.

→ On the **Quick Access Toolbar** page of the **Excel Options** dialog box, in the **Customize Quick Access Toolbar** pane, click the command. Then click the **Remove** button.

> ➤ **To change the order of commands on the Quick Access Toolbar**

→ On the **Quick Access Toolbar** page of the **Excel Options** dialog box, in the **Customize Quick Access Toolbar** pane, click the command you want to move. Then click **Move Up** to move the command to the left or **Move Down** to move it to the right.

➤ **To separate commands on the Quick Access Toolbar**

→ In the **Customize Quick Access Toolbar** pane, click the command after which you want to insert a separator. At the top of the **Choose commands** pane, click **<Separator>**. Then click **Add**.

➤ **To create a Quick Access Toolbar that is specific to the current workbook**

→ On the **Quick Access Toolbar** page of the **Excel Options** dialog box, in the **Customize Quick Access Toolbar** list, click **For** *document name*. Then add buttons to the toolbar as usual.

➤ **To change the location of the Quick Access Toolbar**

→ On the **Customize Quick Access Toolbar** menu, click **Show Below the Ribbon** or **Show Above the Ribbon**.

→ Right-click the **Quick Access Toolbar**, and then click **Show Quick Access Toolbar Below the Ribbon** or **Show Quick Access Toolbar Above the Ribbon**.

→ On the **Quick Access Toolbar** page of the **Excel Options** dialog box, select or clear the **Show Quick Access Toolbar below the Ribbon** check box.

➤ **To reset the Quick Access Toolbar to its default content**

→ On the **Quick Access Toolbar** page of the **Excel Options** dialog box, click the **Reset** button, and then click **Reset only Quick Access Toolbar** or **Reset all customizations**.

> **Tip** Resetting the Quick Access Toolbar doesn't change its location.

Customizing the ribbon

Experienced users who upgrade to Excel 2013 might identify a few commands that no longer seem to be available. Lesser-used commands do not appear on the ribbon; instead, they are hidden in dialog boxes or panes, or not available at all from the standard user interface. You can make any of these commands easily accessible by adding it to the Quick Access Toolbar or to the ribbon.

You can customize the ribbon to display more or fewer tabs and groups of commands. You can choose from among all commands that are available in the program to create custom tabs and groups of commands.

While working in the program window, you can minimize the ribbon to increase the available working space. The minimized ribbon displays only the tab names.

➤ **To modify the ribbon tabs and groups**

1. Display the **Customize Ribbon** page of the **Excel Options** dialog box.

2. In the **Customize the Ribbon** list, click the group of tabs on which you want to modify content.

3. In the **Customize the Ribbon** pane, do any of the following:

   ○ To prevent a tab from appearing on the ribbon, clear the check box that precedes the tab name.

   ○ To allow a tab to appear on the ribbon, select the check box that precedes the tab name.

   ○ To remove a group from a tab, click the **Expand** button that precedes the tab name to display its groups, click a group name, and then click the **Remove** button.

   > **Tip** The group is removed only from the tab, not from the program.

   ○ To change the display name of a built-in tab or group, click the tab name or group name, and then click the **Rename** button. In the **Rename** dialog box, enter the name you want in the **Display name** box, and then click **OK**.

   ○ To move a group of commands to another tab, expand the source and destination tabs, and click the group you want to move. Then drag the group to its new location or click the **Move Up** or **Move Down** button until the group is where you want it.

➤ **To add a custom tab to the ribbon**

1. On the **Customize Ribbon** page of the **Excel Options** dialog box, in the **Customize the Ribbon** pane, select the tab after which you want the new tab to appear. Then click the **New Tab** button.

2. Click **New Tab (Custom)**, and then click the **Rename** button.

3. In the **Rename** dialog box, enter the name you want to assign to the custom tab in the **Display name** box, and then click **OK**.

> **Tip** Built-in tab names appear in uppercase letters, but you can use uppercase and lowercase letters when naming custom tabs and groups. You might want to use capitalized names to differentiate custom tabs from built-in tabs.

➤ **To add a custom group to a tab**

1. In the **Customize the Ribbon** pane, select the tab on which you want the group to appear, and then click the **New Group** button.

2. Click **New Group (Custom)**, and then click the **Rename** button.

3. In the **Rename** dialog box, click the icon that you want to appear when the custom group is condensed. In the **Display name** box, enter the name you want to assign to the custom group. Then click **OK**.

➤ **To add a command to a custom group**

1. In the **Customize the Ribbon** pane, click the custom group to which you want to add the command.

2. In the **Choose commands from** list, click the group of commands from which you want to select.

3. In the **Choose commands** pane, locate the command you want to add, and then click the **Add** button.

> **Tip** You can add commands to and remove commands from custom groups but not from predefined groups.

➤ **To remove a command from a custom group**

→ In the **Customize the Ribbon** pane, click the command. Then click the **Remove** button.

➤ **To reset a tab or the ribbon to its default content and configuration**

→ On the **Customize Ribbon** page of the **Excel Options** dialog box, click the **Reset** button, and then click **Reset only selected Ribbon tab** or **Reset all customizations**.

Working with macros

Macros are useful for completing repetitive tasks or tasks that you perform frequently. You can record a series of simple actions that you perform in Excel and save the recorded actions as a macro. If you want to automate a more advanced task and have some basic coding skills, you can record the basic actions and then modify the code in the recorded macro to meet your needs.

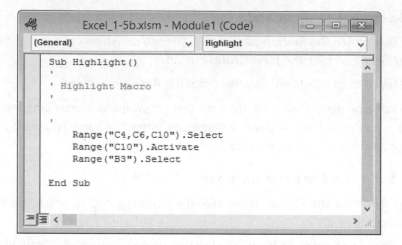

Macros can be saved in macro-enabled workbooks and macro-enabled templates. They cannot be saved in standard Excel workbooks or templates. You can control the way Excel handles macros from the Macro Settings page of the Trust Center.

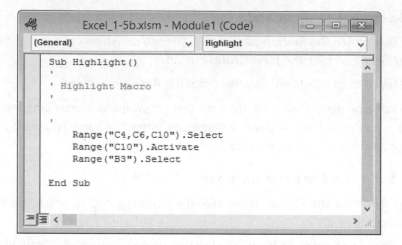

➤ To record a macro

1. On the **View** tab, click the **Macros** arrow, and then click **Record Macro**.

2. In the **Record Macro** dialog box, enter a name for the macro in the **Macro name** box (the name cannot include spaces) and a description of its actions in the **Description** box.

3. In the **Store macro in** list, click the template or workbook in which you want to save the macro.

4. If you want to assign the macro to a keyboard shortcut, enter any one letter (uppercase or lowercase) in the box after **Ctrl+** in the **Shortcut key** area.

5. Click **OK**, and then perform each step of the task you want to record as a macro. A white square near the left end of the status bar indicates that Excel is recording.

> **Tip** You can perform the task by clicking commands or by pressing buttons.

6. When you complete the task, click the status bar indicator to stop recording, or click the **Macros** arrow, and then click **Stop Recording**.

➤ **To modify a macro**

1. On the **View** tab, click the **Macros** button (or press **Alt+F8**).

2. In the **Macros** dialog box, click the name of the macro you want to modify, and then click **Edit**.

3. In the **Microsoft Visual Basic for Applications** window, select the macro you want to modify, and then edit the code.

Modifying workbook properties

Before distributing a workbook, you might want to attach properties to it so that the file is readily identifiable in the Details view of any browsing dialog box, such as the Open dialog box. In Excel 2013, workbook properties are easily accessible from the Info page of the Backstage view. You can view and modify some properties directly on the Info page, or you can work in the Document Panel or Properties dialog box.

➤ **To set or change a basic property**

→ On the **Info** page of the **Backstage** view, click the property to activate it, and then add or change information.

➤ **To display additional common properties**

→ On the **Info** page of the **Backstage** view, click **Show All Properties**.

➤ **To display all properties in the Properties dialog box**

→ On the **Info** page of the **Backstage** view, click **Properties**, and then click **Advanced Properties**.

→ In File Explorer, right-click the file, and then click **Properties**.

> **Tip** In Windows 8, File Explorer replaced Windows Explorer. Throughout this book, we refer to this utility by its Windows 8 name. If your computer is running Windows 7 or an earlier version of Windows, use Windows Explorer instead.

Properties ˅

Size	32.8KB
Title	2013 Argyle Drill Team
Tags	AYSA, Youth Sports
Comments	Add comments
Template	
Status	Waiting for input
Categories	Add a category
Subject	Drill team participants
Hyperlink Base	Add text
Company	Specify the company

Related Dates

Last Modified	Yesterday, 9:57 PM
Created	7/11/2013 7:18 PM
Last Printed	Yesterday, 9:45 PM

Related People

Manager	Specify the manager
Author	Add an author
Last Modified By	Joan Lambert

Related Documents

Open File Location

Show Fewer Properties

➤ To display properties in the Document Panel

1. On the **Info** page of the **Backstage** view, click **Properties**, and then click **Show Document Panel**.

2. In the **Document Information Panel**, click the **Property Views and Options** button, and then click **Document Properties – Server** to display properties associated with a server version of the document (for example, properties used in a document workspace), **Document Properties** to display the common properties stored with the document, or **Advanced Properties** to display the Properties dialog box.

> **Tip** In the Document Panel, fields marked with a red asterisk are required. Required fields are usually associated with the requirements of a Microsoft SharePoint document library in which the workbook is saved.

Practice tasks

The practice files for these tasks are located in the MOSExcel2013\Objective1 practice file folder. Save the results of the tasks in the same folder.

- Open the *Excel_1-4a* workbook, and complete the following tasks:
  - ○ Hide the column containing the Inventory ID, and the row containing the data's source notes. Then unhide the row but not the column.
  - ○ Add the Calculator button (which is not available on any ribbon tab) to the Quick Access Toolbar, make it the leftmost button, and visually separate it from the other buttons.
  - ○ Create a Quick Access Toolbar for only the current workbook that contains buttons for inserting pictures, charts, and tables. Then display the Quick Access Toolbar below the ribbon.
  - ○ Reset the Quick Access Toolbar to its default content, and display it above the ribbon.

- Open the *Excel_1-4b* workbook, and complete the following tasks:
  - ○ On the Personal Monthly Budget worksheet, freeze rows 1 through 9 so that when you scroll the rest of the workbook, those rows are always visible. Then unfreeze the panes.
  - ○ Split the Personal Monthly Budget worksheet vertically so that you can display rows 1 through 9 in the top window and scroll the budget data in the bottom window.
  - ○ Attach the keywords *spending* and *saving* to the workbook.
  - ○ Display the Personal Monthly Budget worksheet in Page Layout view, and then zoom out so you can see the entire first page.
  - ○ Select the Projected Monthly Income section of the worksheet, and zoom in to display only the selected cells.

- In the *Excel_1-4c* workbook, hide the By Product-Customer Filtered worksheet.

1.5 Configure worksheets and workbooks to print or save

Printing workbook content

An Excel workbook can contain many separate worksheets of data. You can print part or all of an individual worksheet, a selected worksheet, or all the worksheets that contain content at one time. By default, Excel prints only the currently active worksheet or worksheet group.

If you want to print only part of a worksheet, you can do so from the Print page of the Backstage view or, if you will often print the same portion of a worksheet, you can define that portion as the print area.

After defining the print area of a workbook, you can add selected ranges to it. A range that is contiguous to the original range becomes part of the original print area definition; a range that is noncontiguous or a different shape becomes a separate print area and is printed on a separate page. You can also remove ranges from the print area.

If you don't want to limit printing to the print area, you can permanently clear the print area or temporarily ignore it by selecting an option on the Print page of the Backstage view.

If your worksheet content doesn't fit naturally within the space allocated to it on the page, you can scale the content for the purpose of printing, instead of modifying the content to make it fit. You can scale the worksheet manually or allow Excel to scale it for you by specifying the number of pages you want the printed worksheet to be.

➤ **To print all populated worksheets in a workbook**

→ On the **Print** page of the **Backstage** view, in the first list in the **Settings** area, click **Print Entire Workbook**.

➤ **To print a single worksheet**

1. Display the worksheet you want to print.

2. On the **Print** page of the **Backstage** view, in the **Settings** area, click **Print Active Sheets** in the first list.

➤ **To print specific worksheets**

1. Group the worksheets that you want to print.

2. On the **Print** page of the **Backstage** view, in the **Settings** area, click **Print Active Sheets** in the first list.

➤ **To print a portion of a worksheet without defining a print area**

1. On the worksheet, select the range of cells you want to print.

2. On the **Print** page of the **Backstage** view, in the **Settings** area, click **Print Selection** in the first list.

➤ **To define a selected range as the print area**

→ On the **Page Layout** tab, in the **Page Setup** group, click the **Print Area** button, and then click **Set Print Area**.

➤ **To add a selected range to a defined print area**

→ On the **Page Layout** tab, in the **Page Setup** group, click the **Print Area** button, and then click **Add to Print Area**.

> **Tip** The Add To Print Area option will not display if the area of the worksheet designated as the print area is currently selected.

➤ **To remove a range from the print area**

1. On the **Page Layout** tab, click the **Page Setup** dialog box launcher.

2. On the **Sheet** page of the **Page Setup** dialog box, change the range reference in the **Print area** box, and then click **OK**.

➤ **To clear the print area**

→ On the **Page Layout** tab, in the **Page Setup** group, click the **Print Area** button, and then click **Clear Print Area**.

➤ **To ignore the print area**

→ On the **Print** page of the **Backstage** view, in the **Settings** area, click **Ignore Print Area** in the first list.

> **Tip** The Ignore Print Area setting remains active (indicated by a check mark) until you turn it off by clicking it again.

➤ **To scale the worksheet when printing**

→ On the **Print** page of the **Backstage** view, in the **Settings** area, click **No Scaling**, and then click **Fit Sheet on One Page**, **Fit All Columns on One Page**, or **Fit All Rows on One Page**.

Or

1. On the **Print** page of the **Backstage** view, in the **Settings** area, click **No Scaling**, and then click **Custom Scaling Options**.

2. On the **Page** page of the **Page Setup** dialog box, do one of the following:

   ○ In the **Scaling** area, click **Adjust to**, and then set the **% normal size** to any number from 10 to 95 percent (in five percent increments).

   ○ In the **Scaling** area, click **Fit to**. Then specify the number of pages horizontally and vertically across which you want to print the worksheet.

3. In the **Page Setup** dialog box, click **OK**.

Saving workbooks

You can save a workbook in multiple locations and in multiple formats.

Where once it was common only to save a file locally on your computer, many people now save files to shared locations such as SharePoint sites, Microsoft SkyDrive folders, and corporate SkyDrive Pro folders for the purpose of collaborating with other people or accessing the files from multiple computers and devices.

You can save a workbook to disk (to your local computer, a network location, or writable media), to an Internet location (a SkyDrive folder or corporate SkyDrive Pro folder), or to a SharePoint site.

Tip With a free SkyDrive account, you can store and share 7 GB (or more) of files, such as photos and Office documents, on the Internet. To create a SkyDrive folder, visit *skydrive.live.com*, and sign in with your Microsoft account.

Book1 - Excel

? – □ ×

Joan Lambert ▾

Save As

⑤ Microsoft

☁ Joan Lambert's SkyDrive

🌐 Other Web Locations

💻 Computer

➕ Add a Place

Add a Place

You can add locations to make it easier to save Office documents to the cloud.

⑤ Office 365 SharePoint

☁ SkyDrive

Info

New

Open

Save

Save As

Print

Share

Export

Close

Account

Options

The 2007 Microsoft Office system introduced a new set of file formats based on XML, called Microsoft Office Open XML Formats. By default, Excel 2013 workbooks are saved in the .xlsx format, which is an Excel-specific Open XML format. The .xlsx format provides the following benefits:

- File sizes are smaller than with previous file formats.
- It is simpler to recover damaged content because XML files can be opened in a variety of text editors.
- Security is greater because .xlsx files cannot contain macros, and personal data can easily be identified and removed from files.

Other Excel-specific Open XML formats include .xlsm for macro-enabled workbooks and .xlsb for binary workbooks.

Workbooks saved in the .xlsx format can be opened by Excel 2013, Excel 2010, and Excel 2007. Users of earlier versions of Excel can download a converter that they can use to open an .xlsx file in their version of Excel.

In addition to saving a workbook for use with Excel 2013, you can save it in other formats, including the following:

- **Excel Macro-Enabled Workbook** To be able to store VBA macro code or Excel 4.0 macro sheets, use the XML-based .xlsm format.

- **Excel 97-2003** To share an Excel workbook with users of an earlier version of Excel, you can save it in the .xls file format.

- **Single File Web Page or Web Page** You can convert a workbook into HTML so that it can be viewed in a web browser. Saving a workbook in the Single File Web Page format creates one .mht or .mhtml file that contains the content and supporting information, whereas saving a workbook in the Web Page format creates one .htm or .html file that sets up the display structure and a folder that contains separate content and supporting information files.

- **Excel Template** To be able to use a workbook as the starting point for other workbooks, you can save the file as a template.

- **Text (Tab delimited) or CSV (Comma delimited)** If you don't know what program will be used to open the file, you can save it as a delimited text file that can be opened by many programs.

> **Tip** When you save a workbook in one of the text formats, you lose all formatting.

If you intend to share an Excel workbook specifically with users of Excel 2003 or earlier, you can save it in the .xls file format used by those versions of the program. Users of Excel 2013, Excel 2010, and Excel 2007 can open an .xls file in Compatibility Mode. Compatibility Mode turns off advanced program features. These features can be re-enabled by saving the file in one of the current file formats.

If you want to ensure that the appearance of the file content is the same no matter what computer or device it is displayed on, you can save it in one of the following formats:

- **Portable Document Format (PDF)** A fixed-layout document format created by Adobe Systems. A PDF file includes the text, fonts, images, and vector graphics that compose the document. The Adobe Reader or Adobe Acrobat software is required to view a PDF document.

- **XML Paper Specification (XPS) document format** A fixed-layout document format created by Microsoft. The XPS document format consists of structured XML markup that defines the layout of a document and the visual appearance of each page, along with rendering rules for distributing, archiving, rendering, processing, and printing the documents.

Each of these formats displays content in a device-independent manner. When saving a workbook in one of these formats, you can specify the content that you want to include in the file.

Options dialog box with the following settings:

Page range
- ◉ All
- ○ Page(s) From: [1] To: [1]

Publish what
- ○ Selection   ○ Entire workbook
- ◉ Active sheet(s)   ○ Table
- ☐ Ignore print areas

Include non-printing information
- ☑ Document properties
- ☑ Document structure tags for accessibility

PDF options
- ☐ ISO 19005-1 compliant (PDF/A)

[OK]   [Cancel]

> **Strategy** Ensure that you are familiar with the types of file formats in which you can save Excel workbooks and when it is appropriate to use each one.

➤ To save a document to a remote location

1. On the **Save As** page of the **Backstage** view, click the type of remote location in which you want to save the file.

2. In the remote location list, click the folder in which you want to save the file, or click **Browse** and then enter your credentials for the remote location.

3. In the **Save As** dialog box, navigate to an existing folder or create a new folder, modify the name in the **File name** box if necessary, and then click **Save**.

> **Tip** You can share a file with other people while saving it to a shared remote location by selecting options on the Share page of the Backstage view.

➤ **To add a SharePoint site that is not associated with Office 365 to your Web Locations list**

1. On the **Save As** page of the **Backstage** view, click **Other Web Locations**, and then click **Browse**.

2. In the **Save As** dialog box, enter the URL of the SharePoint site in the **Address** bar, and then click the **Go to** button.

3. Enter your user credentials for the SharePoint site, and then click **OK**.

➤ **To add an Office 365 SharePoint site or SkyDrive to your Save As locations**

1. On the **Save As** page of the **Backstage** view, click **Add a Place**.

2. In the **Add a Place** list, click **Office 365 SharePoint** or **SkyDrive**.

3. In the **Add a service** window, enter the email address with which you sign in to the SharePoint site or SkyDrive, and then click **Next**.

4. In the **Sign In** window, enter your user credentials for the SharePoint site or SkyDrive, and then click **Sign in**.

➤ **To set browser view options when saving a workbook to a SharePoint site**

1. In the **Save As** dialog box, browse to the document library in which you want to save the file. Enter a file name and select a file format.

2. To specify the workbook content that will be displayed when the workbook is viewed in the browser, click **Browser View Options**.

3. On the **Show** page of the **Browser View Options** dialog box, in the list, do one of the following, and then click **OK**:

   ○ Click **Entire Workbook** to make all sheets and objects available for display in the browser.

   ○ Click **Sheets**, and then select the check boxes of the worksheets or object sheets you want to make available for display.

   ○ Click **Items in the Workbook**, and then display the check boxes of the workbook objects you want to make available for display.

4. In the **Save As** dialog box, click **Save**.

➤ **To save a workbook in a specific format**

1. From the **Save As** page of the **Backstage** view, select the location in which you want to save the workbook.

2. In the **Save As** dialog box, enter a file name and select a file format, and then click **Save**.

Or

1. On the **Export** page of the **Backstage** view, click **Create PDF/XPS Document** in the left pane, and then click **Create PDF/XPS** in the right pane.

2. In the **Publish as PDF or XPS** dialog box, browse to the folder in which you want to save the workbook, and enter a file name.

3. In the **Optimize for** area, click **Standard** to generate a larger, higher-quality file or **Minimum size** to generate a smaller, lower-quality file. Then click **Options**.

4. In the **Options** dialog box, select the workbook content you want to include in the file, and then click **OK**.

5. In the **Publish as PDF or XPS** dialog box, click **Publish**.

Or

1. On the **Export** page of the **Backstage** view, click **Change File Type**, and click the file format in which you want to save the workbook. Then click the **Save As** button.

2. In the **Save As** dialog box, browse to the folder in which you want to save the workbook. Enter a file name, and then click **Save**.

Practice tasks

The practice files for these tasks are located in the MOSExcel2013\Objective1 practice file folder. Save the results of the tasks in the same folder.

- Open the *Excel_1-5a* workbook, and configure the worksheet so that printing with the default settings prints only columns B and C, and the worksheet gridlines print.

- Open the *Excel_1-5b* macro-enabled workbook, and save it with the file name *MOS-Compatible* in a file format that can be viewed and worked on by a colleague who is using Excel 2003.

- Save the *MOS-Compatible* workbook with the file name *MOS-Template* in a file format that can be used as the basis for other similar workbooks in the future.

- Save the *MOS-Template* workbook with the file name *MOS-Macro* in a file format that permits users to run the macro that is saved in the workbook.

Objective review

Before finishing this chapter, ensure that you have mastered the following skills:

1.1   Create workbooks and worksheets

1.2   Navigate through worksheets and workbooks

1.3   Format worksheets and workbooks

1.4   Customize options and views for worksheets and workbooks

1.5   Configure worksheets and workbooks to print or save

2 Manage cells and ranges

The skills tested in this section of the Microsoft Office Specialist exam for Microsoft Excel 2013 relate to managing cells and cell ranges in worksheets and workbooks. Specifically, the following objectives are associated with this set of skills:

2.1 Insert data in cells and ranges

2.2 Format cells and ranges

2.3 Order and group cells and ranges

Excel stores data in individual cells of the worksheets within a workbook. You can process or reference the data in each cell in many ways; either individually or in logical groups. An organized set of contiguous data is a *data range*. A data range can be as small as a list of dates, or as large as a multicolumn table that has thousands of rows of data. If you apply an Excel table format to a data range, it then becomes a table, which has additional functionality beyond that of a data range. We discuss tables in Chapter 3, "Manage tables." The functionality in this chapter explicitly pertains to data ranges that are not formatted as Excel tables.

You might populate a worksheet from scratch or by creating, reusing, or calculating data from other sources. You can perform various operations on data when pasting it into a worksheet, either to maintain the original state of the data or to change it. When creating data from scratch, you can quickly enter large amounts of data that follows a pattern by filling a numeric or alphanumeric data series. You can fill any of the default series that come with Excel or create a custom data series.

This chapter guides you in studying ways of working with the content, appearance, and functionality of cells and data ranges.

> **Practice Files** To complete the practice tasks in this chapter, you need the practice files contained in the MOSExcel2013\Objective2 practice file folder. For more information, see "Download the practice files" in this book's Introduction.

2.1 Insert data in cells and ranges

Creating data

The most basic method of inserting data in cells is by entering it manually. When you create the structure of a data range, or a series of formulas, you can automate the process of completing data patterns (such as *January*, *February*, *March*) or copying calculations from one row or column to those adjacent. Automation saves time and can help prevent human errors.

You can quickly fill adjacent cells with data that continues a formula or a series of numbers, days, or dates, either manually from the Fill menu, or automatically by dragging the fill handle. When copying or filling data by using the Fill menu commands, you can set specific options in the Series dialog box for the pattern of the data sequence you want to create.

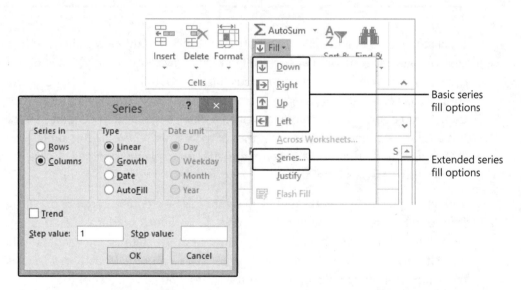

When creating a series based on one or more selected cells (called *filling a series*), you can select from the following series types:

- **Linear** Excel calculates the series values by adding the value you enter in the Step Value box to each cell in the series.

- **Growth** Excel calculates the series values by multiplying each cell in the series by the step value.

- **Date** Excel calculates the series values by incrementing each cell in the series of dates, designated by the Date Unit you select, by the step value.

- **AutoFill** This option creates a series that produces the same results as dragging the fill handle.

When using the AutoFill feature, either from the Fill menu or by dragging the fill handle, the Auto Fill Options button appears in the lower-right corner of the fill range. Clicking the button displays a menu of fill options. The fill options vary based on the type of content being filled.

Fill handle

Auto Fill Options button

Auto Fill Options menu

Tip The Auto Fill Options button does not appear when copying data to adjacent cells.

You can use the AutoFill feature to create sequences of numbers, days, and dates; to apply formatting from one cell to adjacent cells; or, if you use Excel for more sophisticated purposes, to create sequences of data generated by formulas, or custom sequences based on information you specify.

If you want to fill a series of information that does not match the available series type or unit, you can create a custom fill series consisting of a specific list of data you want your series to conform to. For example, this could be a list of names, regions, or industry-specific reference points.

You can also use the fill functionality to copy text or numeric data within the column or row.

[A screenshot of an Options dialog box with the Custom Lists tab selected.]

Options

Custom Lists

Custom lists:

NEW LIST
Sun, Mon, Tue, Wed, Thu, Fri, :
Sunday, Monday, Tuesday, We
Jan, Feb, Mar, Apr, May, Jun, Ju
January, February, March, Apri
Spring, Summer, Autumn, Win

List entries:

Spring
Summer
Autumn
Winter

Add

Delete

Press Enter to separate list entries.

Import list from cells:

$F$5:$F$8

Import

OK   Cancel

➤ **To fill a simple numeric, day, or date series**

1. In the upper-left cell of the range you want to fill, enter the first number, day, or date of the series you want to create.

   Or

   To create a series in which numbers or dates increment by more than one, enter the first two or more values of the series in the first cells of the range you want to fill.

   > **Tip** Enter as many numbers or dates as are necessary to establish the series.

2. Select the cell or cells that define the series.

3. Drag the fill handle down or to the right to create an increasing series.

   Or

   Drag the fill handle up or to the left to create a decreasing series.

   > **Tip** When using the fill handle, you can drag in only one direction at a time; to fill a range of multiple columns and rows, first drag in one direction, then release the mouse button and drag the new fill handle in the other direction. The default fill series value is indicated in a tooltip as you drag.

➤ **To fill a selective day or date series**

1. Fill the series. Immediately after you release the mouse button, click the **Auto Fill Options** button that appears in the lower-right corner of the cell range.

2. On the **Auto Fill Options** menu, click **Fill Days**, **Fill Weekdays**, **Fill Months**, or **Fill Years**.

➤ **To fill a formatted numeric series**

1. Enter the amount or amounts beginning the series.

2. On the **Home** tab, use the commands in the **Number** group to format the amount or amounts as currency, percentage, fraction, or whatever number format you want.

3. Select the cell or cells beginning the series.

4. Drag the fill handle down or to the right to create an increasing series, or up or to the left to create a decreasing series.

5. Click the **Auto Fill Options** button and then, on the **Auto Fill Options** menu, click **Fill Series**.

➤ **To set advanced options for a numeric, day, or date series**

1. Enter the number or date beginning the series, and then select the cell range you want to fill.

2. On the **Home** tab, in the **Editing** group, in the **Fill** list, click **Series**.

3. In the **Series** dialog box, select the options you want, and then click **OK**.

➤ **To exclude formatting when filling a series**

1. Fill the series, and then click the **Auto Fill Options** button.

2. On the **Auto Fill Options** menu, click **Fill Without Formatting**.

➤ **To create a custom fill series**

1. On the **Advanced** page of the **Excel Options** dialog box, in the **General** area, click the **Edit Custom Lists** button.

2. In the **Custom Lists** dialog box, enter the fill series elements in the **List entries** box, pressing **Enter** after each.

> **Tip** If the fill series elements are already entered on a worksheet, click the worksheet icon in the Import List From Cells box, select the fill series elements, click the icon again, and then click Import to add them to the List Entries box.

3. In the **List entries** list, verify or edit the entries. Click **Add**, and then click **OK** in each of the open dialog boxes.

➤ **To apply a custom fill series**

→ Select a cell containing any entry from the custom list, and then drag the fill handle to create a series.

> **Tip** Excel fills the series with either lowercase or capitalized entries to match the cell you start with.

➤ **To copy text or currency amounts to adjacent cells**

1. In the upper-left cell of the range you want to fill, enter the text or currency amount (formatted as currency) you want to duplicate, and then select the cell.

2. Drag the fill handle up, down, to the left, or to the right to encompass the cell range you want to fill.

➤ **To copy numeric data to adjacent cells**

1. In the upper-left cell of the range you want to fill, enter the value you want to duplicate, and then select the cell.

2. Drag the fill handle up, down, to the left, or to the right to encompass the cell range you want to fill.

   Or

1. In the upper-left cell of the range you want to fill, enter the value you want to duplicate.

2. Select the cell and the entire cell range you want to duplicate the value into.

3. On the **Home** tab, in the **Editing** group, click the **Fill** button, and then in the list, click the first direction in which you want to duplicate the value (**Down** or **Right**).

4. To fill a cell range that includes multiple rows and columns, repeat steps 2 and 3, selecting the other direction.

> **Tip** You can also fill a cell range up or to the left; if you do so, make sure that the value you want to duplicate is in the lower-right cell of the range you want to fill.

➤ **To exclude formatting when filling or copying data**

→ Drag the fill handle to fill the series or copy the data, and then on the **Auto Fill Options** menu, click **Fill Without Formatting**.

Reusing data

If the content you want to work with in Excel already exists elsewhere—in another worksheet, a document, a database table, or displayed on the screen within a report or webpage—you can cut or copy the data from the source location to the Microsoft Office Clipboard and then paste it into the worksheet. When pasting data, you have several options for inserting values, formulas, formatting, or links to the original source data into the new location.

	Days with AQI data	Days AQI was Good	Days AQI was Moderate
4			
5	365	93	150
6	315	219	94
7	365	266	92
8	(Ctrl) ▾	182	116
9	Paste	181	123
10		287	65
11		284	73
12		187	140
13		170	117
14	Paste Values	243	56
15		303	58
16	Other Paste Options	289	42
17		301	64
18		271	90
19	365	306	53

> **Tip** The available paste options vary based on the content being pasted.

Excel also offers some advanced pasting techniques you can use to modify data while pasting it into a worksheet. Using the Paste Special feature, you can perform mathematical operations when you paste data over existing data, you can transpose columns to rows and rows to columns, and you can be selective about what you want to paste from the source cells. You have the option to paste only values, formulas, formatting, data validation, comments, or column widths. You can choose to exclude borders when you paste. You can also link to data rather than inserting it, so that if the source data changes, the copied data will also change.

You can insert cut or copied cell contents into empty cells, or directly into an existing table or data range. When you insert a range of cells rather than an entire row or column, you must also specify where Excel should move the existing content to make room for the new cells.

Tip Always select a single cell when inserting cut or copied cells. If you select a range that is a different size and shape from the one you want to insert, you will get an error message.

Section 1.2, "Navigate through worksheets and workbooks," described methods of locating data and worksheet elements within a workbook. You can use similar methods to replace data within a worksheet. For example, you might reuse existing content by making a copy of a worksheet and updating the year within the worksheet formulas. You can replace content within the sheet or workbook in a single operation.

Unlike the Find operation, which permits you to search formulas, values, or comments, the Replace operation looks only in formulas. It doesn't replace search strings in comments or in calculated values.

> **See Also** For information about formulas, see Chapter 4, "Apply formulas and functions."

➤ To add cells from the Clipboard to a data range

1. Select the upper-left cell of the area into which you want to insert the cut or copied cells.

2. On the **Home** tab, in the **Cells** group, click the **Insert** arrow, and then click **Insert Cells**.

3. In the **Insert Paste** dialog box, click **Shift cells right**, **Shift cells down** to move the existing data. Then click **OK**.

➤ To paste cells from the Clipboard over existing data

1. Select the upper-left cell of the area into which you want to insert the cut or copied cells.

2. On the **Home** tab, in the **Clipboard** group, click **Paste** (or press **Ctrl+V**).

➤ To paste formula results from one cell range to another

1. Select and copy the cell range containing the formulas you want to copy the values from.

2. Select the cell into which you want to copy the first value.

3. On the **Home** tab, in the **Clipboard** group, display the **Paste** list and then, in the **Paste Values** section, click the **Values** button.

➤ **To transpose rows and columns**

1. Select the data range you want to transpose.

2. On the **Home** tab, in the **Clipboard** group, click the **Copy** button.

3. Select the cell into which you want to copy the first value of the transposed data.

4. On the **Home** tab, in the **Clipboard** group, display the **Paste** list and then, in the **Paste** section, click the **Transpose** button.

> **Tip** Transposing data retains its formatting.

➤ **To replace data**

1. On the **Home** tab, in the **Editing** group, display the **Find & Select** list, and then click **Replace** (or press **Ctrl+H**).

2. On the **Replace** page of the **Find and Replace** dialog box, enter the data you want to locate in the **Find what** box, and the replacement data in the **Replace with** box.

3. In the **Within** list, click **Workbook** or **Sheet** to set the scope of the operation.

4. Select the **Match case** or **Match entire cell contents** check boxes if necessary to further refine the search term.

5. Click **Replace All**, or click **Find Next** and then click **Replace** or **Find Next** for each instance of the search term that is located.

Practice tasks

The practice files for these tasks are located in the MOSExcel2013\Objective2 practice file folder. Save the results of the tasks in the same folder.

- Open the *Excel_2-1a* workbook, and complete the following tasks by using the data in cells B4:G9 of the Ad Buy Constraints worksheet:

  - Paste only the values and formatting into the range beginning at B18.

  - Paste only the formulas into the range beginning at B25.

  - Paste only the formatting (but not the content) into the range beginning at B32.

  - Delete rows to move the headings to row 1. Delete columns to move the Magazine column to column A. Cut the data from the Mag3 row (B4:F4) and insert it into the Mag2 row (B3:F3). Move the Cost Per Ad data to the left of the Total Cost cells. Finally, insert two cells in positions B8:B9, shifting any existing data down.

  - Transpose the names in the Magazine column (cells A1:A6) to the first row of a new worksheet.

- Open the *Excel_2-1b* workbook, and complete the following tasks on the Price List worksheet:

  - Using the fill handle, fill cells A2:A21 with *Item 1*, *Item 2*, *Item 3*, and so on through *Item 20*.

  - Fill cells B2:B21 with *10, 20, 30*, and so on through *200*.

  - Then fill cells C2:C21 with *$3.00, $2.95, $2.90*, and so on through *$2.05*.

  - Copy the background and font formatting from cell A1 to cells A2:A21. Then delete the contents of cell A1 (but not the cell).

- Open the *Excel_2-1c* workbook, and complete the following tasks on the Duty Roster worksheet:

  - Fill cells B1:K1 with the days *Monday* through *Friday*, repeated twice.

  - Create a custom series that uses the names entered in cells B2:B7. Fill the series in each row to create a rotating duty roster for the two weeks.

- In the *Excel_2-1d* workbook, on the Term Schedule worksheet, select cells A3:F14. Use the fill functionality to duplicate the selected term schedule and following empty row immediately below the original (through cell F25). Select the correct AutoFill option to ensure that the Period column in the copy of the schedule displays periods 1 through 8.

2.2 Format cells and ranges

Formatting cell structure

Cell formatting can be applied to a cell, a row, a column, or the entire worksheet. However, some kinds of formatting can detract from the readability of a worksheet if they are applied haphazardly. The formatting you might typically apply to a row or column include the following:

- **Text wrapping** By default, Excel does not wrap text in a cell. Instead, it allows the entry to overflow into the surrounding cells (to the right from a left-aligned cell, to the left from a right-aligned cell, and to both sides from a center-aligned cell) if those cells are empty, or hides the part that won't fit if the cells contains content. To make the entire entry visible, you can allow the cell entry to wrap to multiple lines.

> **Tip** Increasing the height of one cell increases the height of the entire row.

- **Alignment** By default, text is left aligned and numbers are right aligned. You can specify a particular horizontal alignment, and you can specify whether multiline entries should start at the top of their cells and go down, be centered, or start at the bottom of their cells and go up.

- **Orientation** By default, entries are horizontal and read from left to right. You can rotate entries for special effect or to allow you to display more information on the screen or a printed page. This capability is particularly useful when you have long column headings above columns of short entries.

Budget drivers	Scenario 1 (Best case)	Scenario 2 (Average case)	Scenario 3 (Worst case)
Probability of shipping on time	98%	95%	90%
Building permits released in last 6 months	25,000	30,000	35,000
Regional economic growth	4%	3%	2%
Competitive strength (products, pricing, promotion, placement)	7	8	9
Probability of key supplier performance	99%	95%	90%

Worksheets that involve data at multiple hierarchical levels often use horizontal and vertical merged cells to clearly delineate relationships. With Excel, you have the following three merge options:

- **Merge & Center** This option merges the cells across the selected rows and columns, and centers the data from the first selected cell in the merged cell.

- **Merge Across** This option creates a separate merged cell for each row in the selection area, and maintains default alignment for the data type of the first cell of each row of the merged cells.

- **Merge Cells** This option merges the cells across the selected rows and columns, and maintains default alignment for the data type of the first cell of the merged cells.

In the case of Merge & Center and Merge Cells, data in selected cells other than the first is deleted. In the case of Merge Across, data in selected cells other than the first cell of each row is deleted.

Merged horizontal cells

Merged vertical cells

	Monday		Tuesday		Wednesday		Thursday		Friday		
	July 15		July 16		July 17		July 18		July 19		
Time In		Total		Total		Total		Total		Total	
Time Out		0.00		0.00		0.00		0.00		0.00	
Meal Break											Total Hours
Time In		Total		Total		Total		Total		Total	
Time Out		0.00		0.00		0.00		0.00		0.00	
Total	0.00		0.00		0.00		0.00		0.00		0.00

You can use the fill functionality to copy text data, numeric data, or cell formatting (such as text color, background color, and alignment) to adjacent cells.

> **Tip** By default, row height is dynamic and increases to fit the text in its cells. If you manually change the height of a row and then change the size or amount of content in that row, you might have to set or reset the row height. For more information about adjusting row height, see "Modifying rows and columns" in section 1.3, "Format worksheets and workbooks."

➤ **To allow the entries in a selected column to wrap**

→ On the **Home** tab, in the **Alignment** group, click the **Wrap Text** button.

➤ **To align the entries of a selected column**

→ On the **Home** tab, in the **Alignment** group, click the **Align Left**, **Center**, or **Align Right** button to specify horizontal alignment, or click the **Top Align**, **Middle Align**, or **Bottom Align** button to specify vertical alignment.

➤ **To change the orientation of a selected row of headings**

→ On the **Home** tab, in the **Alignment** group, click the **Orientation** button, and then click the angle you want in the list.

> **Tip** You can change the text alignment, text control, text direction, and text orientation settings on the Alignment page of the Format Cells dialog box.

➤ **To merge selected cells**

→ On the **Home** tab, in the **Alignment** group, click the **Merge & Center** button to center and bottom-align the entry from the first cell.

→ On the **Home** tab, in the **Alignment** group, display the **Merge & Center** list, and then click **Merge Across** to create a separate merged cell on each selected row, maintaining the horizontal alignment of the data type in the first cell of each row.

→ On the **Home** tab, in the **Alignment** group, display the **Merge & Center** list, and then click **Merge Cells** to merge the entire selection, maintaining the horizontal alignment of the data type in the first cell.

Formatting cell content

By default, the font used for text in a new Excel worksheet is 11-point Calibri, but you can use the same techniques you would use in any Office 2013 program to change the font and the following font attributes:

- Size
- Style
- Color
- Underline

You can change individual attributes from the Font group on the Home tab or from the Mini Toolbar. You can change several attributes at once in the Format Cells dialog box.

Format Cells   ?   ×

| Number | Alignment | Font | Border | Fill | Protection |

Font:

Calibri

T Calibri Light (Headings)
T Calibri (Body)
Adobe Arabic
Adobe Caslon Pro
Adobe Caslon Pro Bold
Adobe Devanagari

Font style:

Regular

Regular
Italic
Bold
Bold Italic

Size:

11

8
9
10
11
12
14

Underline:

None

Color:

☑ Normal font

Effects

☐ Strikethrough
☐ Superscript
☐ Subscript

Preview

AaBbCcYyZz

This is a TrueType font. The same font will be used on both your printer and your screen.

OK   Cancel

You don't have to apply cell formats one at a time. You can quickly apply several formats at once by clicking a style in the Cell Styles gallery. Some of the categories of styles in this gallery are static, whereas others are dynamic and change according to the theme applied to the worksheet.

Good, Bad and Neutral

| Normal | Bad | Good | Neutral |

Data and Model

| Calculation | Check Cell | Explanatory ... | Input | Linked Cell | Note |
| Output | Warning Text |

Titles and Headings

| **Heading 1** | **Heading 2** | Heading 3 | Heading 4 | Title | Total |

Themed Cell Styles

20% - Accent1	20% - Accent2	20% - Accent3	20% - Accent4	20% - Accent5	20% - Accent6
40% - Accent1	40% - Accent2	40% - Accent3	40% - Accent4	40% - Accent5	40% - Accent6
60% - Accent1	60% - Accent2	60% - Accent3	60% - Accent4	60% - Accent5	60% - Accent6
Accent1	Accent2	Accent3	Accent4	Accent5	Accent6

Number Format

| Comma | Comma [0] | Currency | Currency [0] | Percent |

New Cell Style...
Merge Styles...

If you need a style that is not already defined, you can manually format a cell and then save the combination of formatting as a cell style that you can easily apply elsewhere.

Style	?	×

S̲tyle name: Product Name

Fo̲rmat...

Style Includes (By Example)

☑ **N̲umber**   General

☑ **A̲lignment**   Horizontal Center, Bottom Aligned

☑ **F̲ont**   Calibri (Body) 12, Bold Accent 5

☑ **B̲order**   Bottom Border

☑ **Fi̲ll**   No Shading

☑ **P̲rotection** Locked

OK	Cancel

➤ **To apply a style to a selected cell**

   1. On the **Home** tab, in the **Styles** group, click the **Cell Styles** button.

   2. In the **Cell Styles** gallery, click the style you want.

➤ **To create a cell style based on a formatted cell**

   1. Select a cell that has the combination of formatting you want to save as a style.

   2. In the **Cell Styles** gallery, click **New Cell Style**.

   3. In the **Style** dialog box, name the style, clear the check boxes of any elements you don't want to include in the style, and then click **OK**.

➤ **To create a cell style from scratch**

   1. In the **Cell Styles** gallery, click **New Cell Style**.

   2. In the **Style** dialog box, enter a name for the style in the **Style name** box.

   3. Click **Format**. In the **Format Cells** dialog box, on the **Number**, **Alignment**, **Font**, **Border**, **Fill**, and **Protection** pages, specify the properties of the custom cell style.

   4. Click **OK** in each of the open dialog boxes.

Applying number formats

By default, all the cells in a new worksheet are assigned the General format. When setting up a worksheet, you assign to cells the format that is most appropriate for the type of information you expect them to contain. The format determines not only how the information looks but also how Excel can work with it.

> **Strategy** Knowing which number formats are appropriate for different types of data is important for efficient worksheet construction. Take the time to explore the formats so that you understand the available options.

You can assign the format before or after you type an entry in the cell. You can also just start typing and have Excel intuit the format from what you type. If you choose the format from the list or allow Excel to assign it for you, the format is applied with its default settings. For number and currency formats, you can change those settings in limited ways by clicking buttons on the Home tab. For all formats, you can change them in more precise ways in the Format Cells dialog box.

If none of the number formats is exactly what you want, you can modify an existing format to define your own. Your format then appears in a list of custom formats so that you can reuse it elsewhere in the workbook.

> **Tip** A custom format is saved in the workbook in which it is created and is not available for other workbooks unless you save the workbook containing the custom format as an Excel template.

> **Strategy** The rules for constructing custom formats are complex. For the exam, you might be asked to modify a format in simple ways, so be sure you are familiar with the characters used in a format and how to represent different types of data and color.

A number format can include up to four sections that correspond to positive numbers, negative numbers, zero values, and text, separated by semicolons, such as the following:

<POSITIVE>;<NEGATIVE>;<ZERO>;<TEXT>

You don't have to include all the sections in the format, but you must include semicolons if you leave a section blank. For example, you could configure the following custom formatting:

[Blue]#,##0.00_);[Red](#,##0.00);0.00;"Test "@

This would result in the display shown in the following table, based on the value entered.

Value entered	Value displayed
123 (positive)	123.00 (blue text, right aligned, moved one space left)
-123 (negative)	(123.00) (red text, right aligned)
0 (zero)	0.00 (default font color, right aligned)
One (text)	Test One (default font color, left aligned)

> **See Also** For a full list of characters that are valid in a custom number format, see the Excel Help topic "Create or delete a custom number format."

Format Cells

Number | Alignment | Font | Border | Fill | Protection

Category:

General
Number
Currency
Accounting
Date
Time
Percentage
Fraction
Scientific
Text
Special
Custom

Sample

Type:

$#,##0.00_);[Red]($#,##0.00)

```
#,##0_);[Red](#,##0)
#,##0.00_);(#,##0.00)
#,##0.00_);[Red](#,##0.00)
$#,##0_);($#,##0)
$#,##0_);[Red]($#,##0)
$#,##0.00_);($#,##0.00)
$#,##0.00_);[Red]($#,##0.00)
0%
0.00%
0.00E+00
##0.0E+0
```

Delete

Type the number format code, using one of the existing codes as a starting point.

OK | Cancel

➤ **To apply a default number format to selected cells**

→ On the **Home** tab, in the **Number** group, display the **Number Format** list, and then click a format.

Tip If you want a number to be treated as text, apply the text format.

➤ **To refine a number or currency format**

→ On the **Home** tab, in the **Number** group, click buttons to add a currency symbol, percent sign, or comma; or to increase or decrease the number of decimal places.

Or

1. On the **Home** tab, click the **Number** dialog box launcher.

2. On the **Number** page of the **Format Cells** dialog box, with the format selected in the **Category** list, adjust the settings, and then click **OK**.

➤ **To apply a custom number format to selected cells**

1. On the **Number** page of the **Format Cells** dialog box, in the **Category** list, click **Custom**.

2. In the **Type** list, select a format that is close to the one you want, and then in the **Type** box, modify the format to meet your needs. Then click **OK**.

➤ **To delete a custom format**

1. On the **Number** page of the **Format Cells** dialog box, in the **Category** list, click **Custom**.

2. In the **Type** list, select the custom format, and then click **Delete**. Then click **OK**.

> **Tip** You cannot delete a built-in format from the Type list.

Copying formatting

You can use the Format Painter tool to copy cell formatting (such as text color, background color, and alignment) to other cells, or the fill functionality to copy formatting to adjacent cells.

➤ **To copy formatting to other cells**

1. Select the cell or cells from which you want to copy formatting.

2. On the **Home** tab, in the **Clipboard** group, click the **Format Painter** button to store the formatting of the selected cell for a single use.

   Or

   In the **Clipboard** group, double-click the **Format Painter** button to store the formatting of the selected cell for multiple uses.

3. Drag the paintbrush-shaped cursor across the cell or cells to which you want to apply the stored formatting.

4. If necessary, click the **Format Painter** button or press **Esc** to turn off the Format Painter tool.

➤ **To copy formatting to adjacent cells**

1. Select the cell that has the formatting you want to copy.

2. Drag the fill handle up, down, to the left, or to the right to encompass the cells you want to format.

3. On the **Auto Fill Options** menu, click **Fill Formatting Only**.

Practice tasks

The practice files for these tasks are located in the MOSExcel2013\Objective2 practice file folder. Save the results of the tasks in the same folder.

- In the *Excel_2-2a* workbook, on the Employees worksheet, merge cells A13:C14 so that the hyperlink is centered in a double-height cell across the three columns.

- Open the *Excel_2-2b* workbook, and complete the following tasks on the Expense worksheet:

  ○ Format the entire worksheet so that all entries wrap in their cells.

  ○ Right-align the entries in column A, and bottom-align the headings in row 9.

  ○ Turn off text wrapping in rows 4, 5, and 9.

  ○ Align the headings in row 9 at a counterclockwise angle.

  ○ Format cell K10 to display its contents in any one of the number formats (Number, Currency, or Accounting) with no decimal places. Then apply the same formatting to cells K11: K23.

  ○ Apply custom number formatting to the TOTAL value in cell K23 (2,643) that will cause it to be displayed in green if it is a positive number or in red if it is a negative number. Do not add formatting for zero or text values. Place a value of *3,000* into the Advances field (cell K22) to verify the formatting of negative numbers.

  ○ Apply the 20% - Accent2 cell style to cells A9:K9.

  ○ Change the font style and size of the cell style applied to cells A9:K9, and then save the formatting combination as a new cell style named *MyStyle*.

2.3 Order and group cells and ranges

Modeling data

Excel worksheets frequently contain vast quantities of numeric data that can be difficult to interpret. Excel provides two useful tools for adding visual keys to data that provide the user with information about how each entry within a data range relates to those around it: conditional formatting and sparklines.

You can make worksheet data easier to interpret by using conditional formatting to format cells based on their values. If a value meets a particular condition, Excel applies the formatting; if it doesn't, the formatting is not applied.

You set up conditional formatting by specifying the condition, which is called a *formatting rule*. You can select from the following types of rules:

- **Highlight cells** Apply formatting to cells that contain data within a specified numeric range, contain specific text, or contain duplicate values.

- **Top/bottom** Apply formatting to cells that contain the highest or lowest values in a range.

- **Data bars** Fill a portion of each cell corresponding to the relationship of the cell's data to the rest of the data in the selected range.

- **Color scales** Fill each cell with a color point from a two-color or three-color gradient that corresponds to the relationship of the cell's data to the rest of the data in the selected range.

- **Icon sets** Insert an icon from a selected set that corresponds to the relationship of the cell's data to the rest of the data in the selected range.

If a predefined formatting rule doesn't meet your needs, you can define a custom rule based on the standard rules, or based on a formula. This provides virtually unlimited opportunities to precisely define conditional formatting.

You can define multiple conditions for the same range of cells or table.

> **Strategy** Familiarize yourself with all the types of rules and their variations so that you know how to quickly apply any condition that might be requested on the exam.

All the rules you create are listed in the Conditional Formatting Rules Manager, in which you can do the following:

- Create, edit, and delete formatting rules.
- Specify the order in which Excel processes formatting rules.
- Specify whether Excel should process additional rules after a cell meets the conditions of a rule.

Conditional Formatting Rules Manager			?	×

Show formatting rules for: This Worksheet ▾

| ⊞ New Rule... | ⊞ Edit Rule... | ✕ Delete Rule | ▲ | ▼ |

Rule (applied in order shown)	Format	Applies to		Stop If True
Data Bar		=$H$14:$L$25	▦	☐
Top 5	AaBbCcYyZz	=$H$14:$L$25	▦	☑
Icon Set	☆ ☆ ☆	=$H$14:$L$25	▦	☐

| OK | Close | Apply |

Sparklines are miniature charts that summarize worksheet data in a single cell. Excel 2013 includes three types of sparklines: Line, Column, and Win/Loss. Line and Column sparklines resemble charts of the same types. A Win/Loss sparkline indicates whether each data point is positive, zero, or negative.

A sparkline consists of a series of markers. Depending on the sparkline type, you can choose to accentuate the first or last point in the data series, the high or low value, or the negative values, by displaying a marker of a different color.

You can apply styles and other formatting to sparklines in the same way that you do to other graphic elements.

11:00 AM	12:00 PM	1:00 PM	2:00 PM	3:00 PM	4:00 PM	5:00 PM	
1687	2391	1486	2075	1626	1326	1612	
1559	2103	2493	1317	1519	1836	1439	
1709	1889	1495	1405	1513	1493	1997	
1811	1479	2339	1839	2416	1838	1403	
2348	1355	1346	1947	2098	1163	1410	
2487	2464	1755	2086	1261	1989	2338	
2211	1195	1395	1727	1171	1753	1029	
1746	2243	1385	1414	1675	2274	1765	
2018	2468	2247	2493	1827	2261	1861	
1936	1233	1677	1988	1690	1649	1784	
1721	2235	1534	1407	1187	1581	2355	

➤ **To quickly apply the default value of a conditional formatting rule**

1. Select the data range you want to format.

2. Click the **Quick Analysis** button that appears in the lower-right corner (or press **Ctrl+Q**) and then click **Data Bars**, **Color Scale**, **Icon Set**, **Greater Than**, or **Top 10%** to apply the default rule and formatting.

➤ **To format font color and cell fill in the selected data range based on a specified condition**

1. On the **Home** tab, in the **Styles** group, click the **Conditional Formatting** button.

2. In the **Conditional Formatting** list, point to **Highlight Cell Rules** or **Top/Bottom Rules**, and then click the type of condition you want to specify.

3. In the dialog box, specify the parameters of the condition, click the formatting combination you want, and then click **OK**.

> **Tip** You can click Custom Format and then specify a combination of number, font, border, and fill formatting.

➤ **To apply formatting based on the relationship of values in the selected data range**

→ In the **Conditional Formatting** list, point to **Data Bars**, **Color Scales**, or **Icon Sets**, and then click the formatting option you want.

> **Tip** You can click More Rules and then specify custom configurations of two-color scales, three-color scales, data bars, or icon sets.

➤ **To create a rule from scratch**

1. In the **Conditional Formatting** list, click **New Rule**.

2. In the **New Formatting Rule** dialog box, in the **Select a Rule Type** list, click the type you want.

3. In the **Edit the Rule Description** area, specify the condition.

4. If the selected conditional formatting rule includes formatting options, click the **Format** button. Then in the **Format Cells** dialog box, specify the number, font, border, and fill formatting to apply if the condition is met, and click **OK**.

5. In the **New Formatting Rule** dialog box, click **OK**.

➤ **To modify the conditional format applied to selected cells**

1. In the **Conditional Formatting** list, click **Manage Rules**.

2. In the **Conditional Formatting Rules Manager** dialog box, click the rule you want to change, and then click **Edit Rule**.

3. In the **Edit Formatting Rule** dialog box, make your changes, and then click **OK**.

➤ **To stop testing the cell for subsequent rules if a rule is met**

→ Open the **Conditional Formatting Rules Manager** dialog box, click the rule, select the **Stop If True** check box, and then click **OK**.

➤ **To delete the conditional format applied to selected cells**

→ In the **Conditional Formatting** list, point to **Clear Rules**, and then click **Clear Rules from Selected Cells** or **Clear Rules from Entire Sheet**.

→ Open the **Conditional Formatting Rules Manager** dialog box, click the rule, click **Delete Rule**, and then click **OK**.

➤ **To create a sparkline or sparklines**

1. Select the data you want to summarize, or click the cell in which you want to insert the sparkline.

2. On the **Insert** tab, in the **Sparklines** group, click **Line**, **Column**, or **Win/Loss** to specify the type of sparkline you want to create.

3. In the **Create Sparklines** dialog box, select, enter, or verify the data range and the location range. Then click **OK**.

➤ **To enhance a sparkline**

→ On the **Design** tool tab, do any of the following:

○ In the **Show** group, select the check boxes for the data markers you want to show, and clear the check boxes for the data markers you want to hide.

○ In the **Style** gallery, click the built-in style you want to apply.

○ In the **Style** group, in the **Sparkline Color** gallery, click the color you want.

○ In the **Style** group, in the **Marker Color** list, in the **Negative Points**, **Markers**, **High Point**, **Low Point**, **First Point**, and **Last Point** galleries, click the colors you want.

➤ **To change the type of a selected sparkline or sparkline group**

→ On the **Design** tool tab, in the **Type** group, click the sparkline type you want.

➤ **To delete a sparkline or sparkline group**

→ Select the sparkline you want to delete. On the **Design** tool tab, in the **Group** group, click the **Clear Selected Sparklines** button.

→ Select one or more sparklines in the sparkline group you want to delete. On the **Design** tool tab, in the **Group** group, click the **Clear Selected Sparklines** arrow, and then click **Clear Selected Sparklines Group**.

Creating named ranges

To simplify the process of creating formulas that refer to a specific range of data, and to make your formulas easier to read and create, you can refer to a cell or range of cells by a name that you define. For example, you might name a cell containing an interest rate *Interest*, or a range of cells containing nonwork days *Holidays*. In a formula, you can refer to a named range by name. Thus you might end up with a formula like this:

=WORKDAY(StartDate,WorkingDays,Holidays)

A formula using named ranges is simpler to understand than its standard equivalent, which could look like this:

=WORKDAY(B2,B$3,Data!B2:B16)

Each named range has a scope, which is the context in which the name is recognized. The scope can be the entire workbook or a specific worksheet. This allows you to use the same name on multiple worksheets. You can include a comment with each name to provide more information about the range. (The comment is visible only in the Name Manager.)

After defining a named range, you can change the range name or the cells included in the named range. You can delete a range name definition from the Name Manager. Note that deleting a cell from a worksheet does not delete any associated range name. Invalid range names are indicated in the Name Manager by #REF! in the Value column.

➤ **To define a selected cell or range of cells as a named range**

→ In the **Name** box at the left end of the **Formula Bar**, enter the range name, and then press **Enter**.

   Or

1. On the **Formulas** tab, in the **Defined Names** group, click the **Define Name** button.

2. In the **New Name** dialog box, enter the range name in the **Name** box.

> **Tip** The New Name dialog box does not indicate any named ranges that the selected cell or cells are already part of.

3. In the **Scope** list, click **Workbook** to define the named range for the entire workbook, or click a specific worksheet name.

4. In the **Comment** box, enter any notes you want to make for your own reference.

5. Verify that the cell or range of cells in the **Refers to** box is correct, and then click **OK**.

> **Tip** If a cell is part of multiple named ranges, only the first name is shown in the Name box. The Name box displays the name of a multiple-cell named range only when all cells in the range are selected.

➤ **To redefine the cells in a named range**

1. On the **Formulas** tab, in the **Defined Names** group, click the **Name Manager** button.

2. In the **Name Manager** window, click the named range you want to change, and then click **Edit**.

3. In the **Edit Name** dialog box, do one of the following, and then click **OK**.

   ○ In the **Refers to** box, enter the cell range to which you want the name to refer.

   ○ If necessary, click the **Minimize** button at the right end of the **Refers to** box to expose the worksheet area. Then on the worksheet, drag to select the cells that you want to include in the named range.

➤ **To change the name of the cells in a named range**

1. In the **Name Manager** window, click the named range you want to change, and then click **Edit**.

2. In the **Edit Name** dialog box, change the range name in the **Name** box, and then click **OK**.

➤ **To delete a named range definition**

→ In the **Name Manager** window, click the named range you want to delete, and click **Delete**. Then click **OK** to confirm the deletion.

Working with data groups and summaries

You can designate specific rows or columns of data within a data range as groups. When you do so, Excel inserts a control, to the left of the row headings or above the column headings, with which you can contract and expand the data group. You can have column groups and row groups on the same worksheet; you cannot have two consecutive groups of rows or columns, they must be separated by one row (the row can contain data). The grouping feature is particularly useful when you're working with a data range or table that is larger than your display because it allows you to easily display and hide groups of columns and rows.

If your data range contains groups of data that are summarized or subtotaled, you can tell Excel to group the data into a maximum of eight levels. In effect, Excel outlines the data, making it possible to hide or display as much detail as you want. After grouping or outlining data, you can expand and collapse groups or levels.

Outline level selectors
Collapsed group

	A	B	C	E	F	H	J
4	Days with AQI data	Days AQI was Good	Days AQI was Moderate	Days AQI was Unhealthy	Maximum AQI value	Median AQI value	State
30	343.68	252.64	72.56	2.48	145.2	41.92	CA Average
31	274	236	38	0	95	33	OR
32	274	236	26	0	135	29	OR
33	273	255	17	0	102	25	OR
34	267	253	14	0	94	9	OR
35	272	245	23.75	0	106.5	24	OR Average
45	361.4	299.7	57.9	0.2	114.3	28.6	WA Average
46	340.3	263.0	63.9	1.7	133.8	36.9	Grand Average

Tip To outline by rows, each column must have a heading in the first row. To outline by columns, each row must have a heading in the first column. In either case, no row or column should be blank.

If your worksheet does not already have summary rows or columns, you can have Excel calculate the summary rows and outline the data in one operation, by using the Subtotal feature. The data range must include headers that identify data subsets, and must be sorted by at least one column that you want to use in the summary. You specify the way the data should be summarized in the Subtotal dialog box. You can use the SUM, COUNT, AVERAGE, MAX, MIN, PRODUCT, COUNT NUMBERS, STDDEV, STDDEVP, VAR, or VARP function to summarize the data of each subset of cells.

Subtotal   ?   ✕

At each change in:

State

Use function:

Average

Add subtotal to:

☑ Days with AQI data
☑ Days AQI was Good
☑ Days AQI was Moderate
☐ Days AQI was Unhealthy for Sensitive Group
☑ Days AQI was Unhealthy
☑ Maximum AQI value

☑ Replace current subtotals
☐ Page break between groups
☑ Summary below data

Remove All   OK   Cancel

After creating subtotals, you can use the controls that appear in the bar to the left of the row headings to collapse and expand subsets of data.

➤ **To create subtotals within a data range**

1. Select the data range and sort it by the column containing the category of data you want to base the subset on.

2. On the **Data** tab, in the **Outline** group, click the **Subtotal** button.

3. In the **Subtotal** dialog box, verify that the correct subtotal category is shown in the **At each change in** list.

4. In the **Use function** list, click the summary function you want to use.

5. In the **Add subtotal to** box, select the check box of each column you want to add subtotals to.

6. Select the check boxes to replace current subtotals, present each data subset on its own page, or summarize the subtotals, and then click **OK**.

➤ **To group worksheet data that contains summary rows or columns**

→ Click any cell in the data. Then on the **Data** tab, in the **Outline** group, click **Auto Outline** in the **Group** list.

Or

1. Click any cell in the subset of data you want to group, and on the **Data** tab, in the **Outline** group, click **Group**.

2. In the **Group** dialog box, click **Rows** or **Columns**, and then click **OK**.

➤ **To hide or display grouped data**

→ In the headings area, click the button representing the outline level you want to display.

> **Tip** Each button displays that level and all those above it.

→ Click a visible group's **Hide Detail** button to hide its rows or columns.

→ Click a hidden group's **Show Detail** button to redisplay its rows or columns.

→ On the **Data** tab, in the **Outline** group, click the **Hide Detail** or **Show Detail** button.

➤ **To ungroup worksheet data**

→ To ungroup a specific group, click any cell in the group, and then on the **Data** tab, in the **Outline** group, click the **Ungroup** button.

→ To ungroup all groups but leave Excel-generated summary rows intact, click any cell in the outline, and then on the **Data** tab, in the **Outline** group, click **Clear Outline** in the **Ungroup** list.

Or

1. To ungroup all groups and remove Excel-generated summary rows, click any cell in the outline, and then on the **Data** tab, in the **Outline** group, click the **Subtotal** button.

2. In the **Subtotal** dialog box, click **Remove All**.

Practice tasks

The practice files for these tasks are located in the MOSExcel2013\Objective2 practice file folder. Save the results of the tasks in the same folder.

- Open the *Excel_2-3a* workbook, and complete the following tasks by using conditional formatting:

  ○ On the Orders worksheet, format Seattle in the City column with red text.

  ○ For all the values in the Extended Price column of the Details worksheet, display the Three Arrows (Colored) icon set. Add blue data bars to the column. Then fill all cells in the column that contain values of more than $100 with bright yellow.

  ○ Configure Excel to first process the rule that fills the cells with yellow, and to not process any more rules for cells that meet this condition.

- Open the *Excel_2-3b* workbook, and complete the following tasks:

  ○ On the JanFeb worksheet, insert a row below the times, and then summarize the data for each *day* of January by using a Column sparkline in that row. Apply the Sparkline Style *Colorful #4* style, and then accentuate the First Point and Last Point data markers.

  ○ Copy the formatted sparkline from January to February.

- On the MarApr worksheet, insert a column to the right of the dates, and then summarize the data for each *hour* by using a Line sparkline in that column. Apply the Sparkline Style Accent 6, Darker 25% style, and then display all the data markers without placing emphasis on any specific type of data marker.

- Copy the formatted sparkline from March to April and ensure that it appears only for the days of the month.

- In the *Excel_2-3c* workbook, on the Results worksheet, define cells A1:T1 as a range named *FirstRow*, and cells A1:A20 as a range named *ColumnA*. Then change the formulas in cells B2:T20 to reference the named ranges.

- Open the *Excel_2-3d* workbook, and complete the following tasks on the Sales By Category worksheet:

  - Have Excel create an outline of the data by adding summary rows that calculate total product sales by category.

  - Add a grouping to hide column A. Then hide all rows other than those containing subtotals.

  - Remove the outline without removing the summary rows.

- Open the *Excel_2-3e* workbook, and complete the following tasks on the Sales By Region worksheet:

  - Create subtotals of sales amounts first by period and then by region.

  - Find the average sales by period and then by region.

  - Find the maximum and minimum sales by period and region.

Objective review

Before finishing this chapter, ensure that you have mastered the following skills:

2.1 Insert data in cells and ranges

2.2 Format cells and ranges

2.3 Order and group cells and ranges

3 Manage tables

The skills tested in this section of the Microsoft Office Specialist exam for Microsoft Excel 2013 relate to creating tables. Specifically, the following objectives are associated with this set of skills:

3.1 Create tables

3.2 Modify tables

3.3 Filter and sort tables

Data stored in an Excel worksheet is organized in rows and columns of cells. Data in a contiguous range of cells is referred to as a *data range*. Similarly, an Excel table is a series of contiguous cells that have been formatted as a named Excel object that has functionality beyond that of a simple data range.

Some table functionality, such as the ability to sort and filter on columns, is also available for data ranges. Useful table functionality that is not available for data ranges includes the automatic application of formatting, the automatic copying of formulas, the ability to perform the following actions:

- Quickly insert column totals or other mathematical results
- Search for the named table object
- Expose the named table object in a web view
- Reference the table or any table field by name in a formula

This chapter guides you in studying methods for creating and modifying tables. It also covers how to filter and sort data that is stored in tables.

> **Practice Files** To complete the practice tasks in this chapter, you need the practice files contained in the MOSExcel2013\Objective3 practice file folder. For more information, see "Download the practice files" in this book's Introduction.

3.1 Create tables

The simplest way to create a table is by converting an existing data range. When you do so, you can retain the existing formatting or apply thematic formatting. You can also create a blank table and then add data to it. (Adding data to a table is often referred to as *populating the table*).

	A	B	C	D	E	F	G	H	I	J	K	L	M
1	Name	Jan	Feb	Mar	Apr	May	Jun	Jul	Aug	Sep	Oct	Nov	Dec
2	Allen	$ 7,222	$ 3,878	$ 5,369	$ 2,763	$ 8,491	$ 5,009	$ 3,956	$ 6,595	$ 8,224	$ 2,790	$ 4,279	$ 3,119
3	Brock	$ 3,008	$ 5,203	$ 7,854	$ 1,201	$ 3,576	$ 2,123	$ 2,416	$ 3,586	$ 4,582	$ 2,679	$ 7,565	$ 4,813
4	Linda	$ 5,311	$ 7,380	$ 1,897	$ 5,736	$ 7,267					$ 6,870	$ 5,171	$ 5,907
5	Max	$ 1,082	$ 4,404	$ 5,274	$ 1,903	$ 7,196					$ 4,097	$ 1,370	$ 4,913
6	Nancy	$ 5,261	$ 4,742	$ 7,706	$ 4,557	$ 4,627					$ 3,053	$ 5,625	$ 4,810
7	Charles	$ 4,280	$ 7,501	$ 3,951	$ 1,824	$ 7,644					$ 3,769	$ 6,708	$ 1,734
8	David	$ 5,098	$ 4,745	$ 5,363	$ 1,438	$ 5,596					$ 1,052	$ 2,804	$ 7,729
9													
10													
11													

Format As Table ? ✕

Where is the data for your table?

=$A$1:$M$8

☑ My table has headers

OK   Cancel

When you create a table, Excel evaluates the table content to identify the cells that are included in the table and define functional table elements (header rows and total rows) and formatting (emphasized columns and banding). Excel assigns a name to the table based on its order of creation in the workbook (*Table1*, *Table2*, and so on). You can change the table name to one that makes it more easily identifiable (such as *2014Sales*, *Students*, or *Products*). When you assign the name, you can also identify the scope whether you want to reference the table by that name in the entire workbook or only in the current worksheet.

Name Manager ? ✕

New...	Edit...	Delete		Filter ▾

Name	Value	Refers To	Scope	Comment
▦ AllGirls	{"Isabella","Ambriz",...	='All Participants'!S...	Workbo...	
▤ Code	#REF!	=#REF!#REF!	Workbo...	
▤ Number	#REF!	=#REF!#REF!	Workbo...	
▤ Overview	{"","","","","","","",""...	=Dashboard!$B$2:...	Workbo...	This page displays...
▤ Phone	#REF!	=#REF!#REF!	Workbo...	
▤ Print_Area	{"","","","","","","",""...	=Dashboard!$B$2:...	Dashbo...	
▦ RedTeam	{"Addy","Chenault",...	='Red Team'!$A$4:...	Workbo...	
▦ SilverTeam	{"Abby Grace","LoB...	='Silver Team'!$A$4...	Workbo...	

Refers to:

✕ ✓   ='All Participants'!$A$2:$U$59

Close

Inserting, deleting, or moving rows or columns in the table automatically updates the table formatting to gracefully include the new content. For example, adding a column to the right end of a table extends the formatting to that column, and inserting a row in the middle of a table that has banded rows updates the banding. You can modify the table element selections at any time.

If you want to remove the table functionality from a table—for example, so you can work with the functionality that is available only for data ranges and not for tables—you can easily convert a table to text. Simply converting the table doesn't remove any table formatting from the table. You can retain the formatting or clear it.

> **See Also** For information about header rows, total rows, emphasized columns, and banding, see section 3.2, "Modify tables." For information about functionality that is specific to data ranges, see Chapter 2, "Manage cells and ranges."

➤ To convert a data range to an unformatted table

1. Click anywhere in the data range.

2. On the **Insert** tab, in the **Tables** group, click **Table**.

3. In the **Create Table** dialog box, do the following, and then click **OK**:

- ○ Verify that the correct data range is displayed in the dialog box (selected in the worksheet).

- ○ Verify that the **My table includes headers** check box is selected if the data range includes headers.

➤ To convert a data range to a formatted table

1. Click anywhere in the data range.

2. On the **Home** tab, in the **Styles** group, click **Format as Table**, and then click the formatting you want.

3. In the **Format As Table** dialog box, do the following, and then click **OK**:

- ○ Verify that the correct data range is displayed in the dialog box (selected in the worksheet).

- ○ Verify that the **My table includes headers** check box is selected if the data range includes headers.

➤ To change the name of a table

→ Click any cell in the table. On the **Design** tool tab, in the **Properties** group, click the table name to select it, and then enter the name you want to assign to the table.

Or

1. Select the table by using one of the following methods:
   - At the left end of the formula bar, click the **Name** arrow, and then click the table name.
   - In the worksheet, drag to select all cells of the table.
2. In the **Name** box on the formula bar or in the **Properties** group on the **Design** tool tab, click the table name to select it. Then enter the name you want to assign to the table.

Or

1. On the **Formulas** tab, in the **Defined Names** group, click **Name Manager**.
2. In the **Name Manager** window, click the table, and then click **Edit**.
3. In the **Edit Name** dialog box, select and replace the table name, and then click **OK**.

➤ **To insert table rows and columns**

→ To add a column to the right end of a table, click in the cell to the right of the last header cell, enter a header for the new column, and then press **Enter**.

→ To insert a single column within a table, click a cell to the left of which you want to add a column. On the **Home** tab, in the **Cells** group, click the **Insert** arrow, and then click **Insert Table Columns to the Left**.

Or

Select a table column to the left of which you want to insert a column, and then in the **Cells** group, click the **Insert** button.

→ To add multiple columns within a table, select the number of columns that you want to insert, and then in the **Cells** group, click the **Insert** button.

→ To add a row at the bottom of the table, click in any cell in the row below the last table row, enter the text for that table cell, and then press **Tab**.

→ To add a row within the table, click a cell above which you want to add a row. On the **Home** tab, in the **Cells** group, click the **Insert** arrow, and then click **Insert Table Rows Above**.

Or

Select a table row above which you want to insert a column, and then in the **Cells** group, click the **Insert** button.

→ To add multiple rows to a table, select the number of rows that you want to insert, and then in the **Cells** group, click the **Insert** button.

➤ **To move rows within a table**

1. Select the table row or rows you want to move, and then do one of the following to cut the selection to the Microsoft Office Clipboard:

   ○ Press **Ctrl+X**.

   ○ Right-click the selection, and then click **Cut**.

   ○ Click **Cut** in the **Clipboard** group on the **Home** tab.

2. Select the table row above which you want to move the cut row or rows.

3. On the **Home** tab, in the **Cells** group, click the **Insert** arrow, and then click **Insert Cut Cells**.

   Or

1. Select the worksheet row or rows containing the table row or rows you want to move, and then cut the selection to the Clipboard.

2. Select the worksheet row above which you want to move the cut row or rows.

3. On the **Home** tab, in the **Cells** group, click the **Insert** arrow, and then click **Insert Cut Cells**.

➤ **To move columns within a table**

→ Point to the top edge of the column you want to move. When the cursor changes to a four-headed arrow, drag the column to the new location (indicated by a thick vertical insertion bar).

   Or

1. Select the worksheet column or columns containing the table column or columns you want to move, and then cut the selection to the Clipboard.

2. Select the worksheet column to the left of which you want to move the cut column or columns.

3. On the **Home** tab, in the **Cells** group, click the **Insert** arrow, and then click **Insert Cut Cells**.

➤ **To delete table rows and columns**

→ Select at least one cell in each row or column you want to delete. On the **Home** tab, in the **Cells** group, click the **Delete** arrow, and then click **Delete Table Rows** or **Delete Table Columns**.

→ Right-click a cell in the row or column you want to delete, click **Delete**, and then click **Table Columns** or **Table Rows**.

➤ **To convert a table to a data range**

→ Right-click the table, click **Table**, and then click **Convert to Range**.

→ Click anywhere in the table. Then on the **Design** tool tab, in the **Tools** group, click **Convert to Range**, and then in the **Microsoft Excel** dialog box, click **Yes**.

Practice tasks

The practice file for these tasks is located in the MOSExcel2013\Objective3 practice file folder. Save the results of the tasks in the same folder.

- Open the *Excel_3-1* workbook, and complete the following tasks on the Sales worksheet:

  ○ Convert the data range A2:M23 to a table that includes a header row. (Retain the existing formatting.)

  ○ Assign the name *Toys2013* to the table.

  ○ Move the *July* column so that it is between the *June* and *August* columns.

  ○ Move the *Linda*, *Max*, and *Nancy* rows at one time so that they are between the *Kay* and *Olivia* rows.

  ○ Add a row to the table for a salesperson named *Raina*, between the *Quentin* and *Steve* rows.

  ○ Add a row to the end of the table for a salesperson named *William*.

  ○ Add a column named *December* to the right end of the table.

3.2 Modify tables

When you create a table, you can apply a combination of formatting elements called a *table style*. The table style includes fonts, borders, and fills that are coordinated to provide a professional appearance. The available table styles are based on the worksheet theme colors. You can change the table style by choosing another from the Table Styles gallery.

> **Tip** If you want to create the table and apply a specific table style at the same time, select the range containing the data, click Format As Table in the Styles group on the Home tab, and then click a style.

The table style governs the appearance of standard cells, special elements, and functional table elements, including the following:

- **Header row** These cells across the top of the table are formatted to contrast with the table content, require an entry, and look like column titles, but are also used to reference fields in formulas.

- **Total row** These cells across the bottom of the table are formatted to contrast with the table content. They do not require an entry, but clicking in any cell displays a list of functions for processing the numeric contents of the table column. These include Average, Count, Count Numbers, Max, Min, Sum, StdDev, and Var, and a link to the Insert Function dialog box from which any function can be inserted in the cell.

Table element formatting is designed to make table entries or fields easier to differentiate, and include an emphasized first column, emphasized last column, banded rows, and banded columns.

➤ **To apply a table style to a selected table**

1. On the **Design** tool tab, in the **Table Styles** group, click the **More** button (if your screen resolution allows for partial display of the **Table Styles** gallery), or click the **Quick Styles** button.

2. In the **Table Styles** gallery, click the style you want.

➤ **To modify functional table elements**

→ On the **Design** tool tab, in the **Table Style Options** group, select or clear the **Header Row**, **Total Row**, or **Filter Button** check boxes.

➤ **To apply contrasting formatting to specific table elements**

→ On the **Design** tool tab, in the **Table Style Options** group, select the **Banded Rows**, **First Column**, **Last Column**, or **Banded Columns** check box.

➤ **To clear formatting from a table**

→ Select any cell in the table. Then on the **Design** tool tab, on the **Table Styles** menu, click **Clear**.

➤ **To clear formatting from a data range**

→ Select the entire data range. On the **Home** tab, in the **Editing** group, click **Clear**, and then click **Clear Formats**.

Practice tasks

The practice file for these tasks is located in the MOSExcel2013\Objective3 practice file folder. Save the results of the tasks in the same folder.

- Open the *Excel_3-2* workbook, and complete the following tasks on the Sales worksheet:
    - ○ Change the table style to a Medium table style of your choice, and then apply banded rows.
    - ○ Configure the table style options to emphasize the first and last columns of the table.
    - ○ Add a total row to the table and change the row name to *Average*. Remove the total from the Year column. For each month, insert the average sales for that month in the row.
- On the Bonuses worksheet, remove the formatting from the ToyBonus table.

3.3 Filter and sort tables

You can easily sort and filter content in an Excel table by using the filter buttons located at the top of each column. If you prefer to hide the filter button, you can do so.

You can sort the values in one or more columns in a worksheet or table in either ascending or descending order. To sort on multiple columns, you specify in the Sort dialog box the order in which you want them to be sorted.

By default, Excel assumes that the first row in the worksheet contains column headings and does not include it in the sort. It also assumes that you want to sort by the values in the table cells. Standard sort orders are from A to Z for text, from smallest to largest for numbers, and from oldest to newest for dates. You can optionally sort by other features of the data range, including cell color, font color, and cell icon. These options are particularly useful in conjunction with conditional formatting.

You can also specify whether entries starting with uppercase and lowercase letters should be sorted separately and the orientation of the sort (whether you want to sort columns or rows).

Tip You can sort a table by the content of hidden columns within that table.

You can sort a data range, but not a table, by rows rather than columns by selecting the Sort Left To Right option. This option is available only when the data range you're sorting contains data that could be sorted in either direction. To successfully sort data from left to right, select a data range that includes only data, and not headers.

Name	January	February	March	April	May	June	July	August
Allen	$ 7,222	$ 3,878	$ 5,369	$ 2,763	$ 8,491	$ 5,009	$ 3,956	$ 6,595
Brock	$ 3,008							
Charles	$ 4,280							
David	$ 1,475							
Emma	$ 2,608							
Frank	$ 3,456							
Grace	$ 6,979							
Heather	$ 1,930							
Irma	$ 1,814							
Joan	$ 5,656							
Kay	$ 4,572							
Linda	$ 5,311							
Max	$ 1,082							
Nancy	$ 5,261							
Olivia	$ 7,030							
Paul	$ 2,144	$ 5,865	$ 2,192	$			7,697	$ 4,837	$ 4,214
Quentin	$ 5,069	$ 3,096	$ 3,341	$	$	2,586	$ 2,270	$ 2,867
Raina	$ 7,690	$ 5,318	$ 2,905	$ 8,582	$ 5,654	$ 6,927	$ 4,403	$ 6,290
Steve	$ 2,253	$ 3,384	$ 3,808	$ 2,151	$ 3,262	$ 8,076	$ 6,282	$ 2,610
Trinity	$ 8,544	$ 7,295	$ 2,119	$ 6,744	$ 7,220	$ 4,523	$ 3,018	$ 6,971

Sort dialog box (overlay):

Add Level | Delete Level | Copy Level | Options... | ☑ My data has headers

Column	Sort On	Order
Sort by: Year	Values	Smallest to Largest
Then by: Name	Values	A to Z

Sort Options (overlay):
☐ Case sensitive
Orientation
◉ Sort top to bottom
◯ Sort left to right
OK | Cancel

When simplifying a table that contains many entries, or when compiling data from multiple sources, you might find that a table contains multiple matching entries. You can easily remove duplicate data from a table by using the Remove Duplicates feature.

Remove Duplicates dialog box:

To delete duplicate values, select one or more columns that contain duplicates.

Select All | Unselect All | ☑ My data has headers

Columns
☑ Product Name
☑ Supplier
☑ Category
☐ Quantity Per Unit
☐ Unit Price

OK | Cancel

> **Tip** Use conditional formatting to locate duplicates so you can review them before permanently deleting them by using the Remove Duplicates feature. If you are uncertain about deleting the duplicate data, copy the original data to another worksheet as a backup.

➤ **To filter data in an Excel table**

1. Click the filter button in the header of the column you want to filter.

2. At the top of the list of column entries, clear the **(Select All)** check box, and then select the check boxes of the items you want to display. Then click **OK**.

> **Tip** You can enlarge the menu to display more options by dragging the handle in the lower-right corner of the menu.

➤ **To remove a filter**

→ Click the filter button, and then click **Clear Filter From** *Column*.

➤ **To sort a table by multiple columns**

1. Click any cell in the range to be sorted. Then on the **Home** tab, in the **Editing** group, click the **Sort & Filter** button, and click **Custom Sort**.

Or

Click any cell in the range to be sorted, and then on the **Data** tab, in the **Sort & Filter** group, click the **Sort** button.

2. In the **Sort** dialog box, click the first column you want in the **Sort by** list. Then click the criteria by which you want to sort in the **Sort on** list. Finally, click the order you want in the **Order** list.

> **Tip** The options in the Sort dialog box change if you click Cell Color, Font Color, or Cell Icon in the Sort On list.

3. Click **Add Level**, and repeat step 2 for the second column. Repeat this step for additional columns.

4. Click **OK**.

➤ **To sort a data range by rows**

→ In the **Sort** dialog box, click **Options**. In the **Sort Option** dialog box, click **Sort left to right**, and then click **OK**.

➤ **To remove duplicate rows from a table**

1. On the **Data** tab, in the **Data Tools** group, click **Remove Duplicates**.

2. In the **Remove Duplicates** dialog box, select the columns from which you want to remove duplicate entries. Then click **OK**.

> **Tip** Remove any outlines or subtotals from your data before trying to remove duplicates.

Practice tasks

The practice files for these tasks are located in the MOSExcel2013\Objective3 practice file folder. Save the results of the tasks in the same folder.

- In the *Excel_3-3a* workbook, on the Bonuses worksheet, apply a filter to display only the bonuses that were less than $2,500.00.

- Open the *Excel_3-3b* workbook, and complete the following tasks on the Sales worksheet:

    ○ Sort the data in ascending order by category and by unit price.

    ○ Sort the data in descending order by category and alphabetically by name.

    ○ Remove duplicates so that there is only one entry for each supplier.

Objective review

Before finishing this chapter, ensure that you have mastered the following skills:

3.1 Create tables

3.2 Modify tables

3.3 Filter and sort tables

4 Apply formulas and functions

The skills tested in this section of the Microsoft Office Specialist exam for Microsoft Excel 2013 relate to the application of functions and formulas. Specifically, the following objectives are associated with this set of skills:

4.1 Utilize cell ranges and references in formulas and functions
4.2 Summarize data by using functions
4.3 Utilize conditional logic in functions
4.4 Format and modify text by using functions

Simple formulas and more complex functions provide the means to interpret raw data stored in a workbook in meaningful ways. They also provide a useful structure for processing information. You can increase the consistency and reliability of information by using formulas to calculate, evaluate, and express data.

You can calculate the data on a worksheet based on data in other areas of the workbook and in other workbooks. Excel maintains referential relationships when you move data or modify the data storage structure.

This chapter guides you in studying ways of referencing cells and ranges of cells both absolutely and relatively in formulas, and using formulas to sum and average cell values and count cells. It also guides you in processing data that meets specific conditions, and in manipulating text by using formulas.

> **Practice Files** To complete the practice tasks in this chapter, you need the practice files contained in the MOSExcel2013\Objective4 practice file folder. For more information, see "Download the practice files" in this book's Introduction.

4.1 Utilize cell ranges and references in formulas and functions

Referencing cells and cell ranges in formulas

Formulas in an Excel worksheet usually involve functions performed on the values contained in one or more other cells on the worksheet (or on another worksheet). A reference that you make in a formula to the contents of a worksheet cell is either a *relative reference*, an *absolute reference*, or a *mixed reference*. It is important to understand the difference and know which to use when creating a formula.

A relative reference to a cell takes the form *A1*. When you copy or fill a formula from the original cell to other cells, a relative reference changes to maintain the relationship between the cell containing the formula and the referenced cell. For example, copying a formula that refers to cell A1 one row down changes the A1 reference to A2; copying the formula one column to the right changes the A1 reference to B1.

An absolute reference takes the form *$A$1*; the dollar sign indicates the absolute reference to column A and an absolute reference to row 1. When you copy or fill a formula from the original cell to other cells, an absolute reference will not change—regardless of the relationship to the referenced cell, the reference stays the same.

	A	B	C	D	E	F
1			Customer	Wingtip Toys		
2			Discount	20%		
3						
4	Product	Toy plane				
5	Base price	$ 15.00				
6						
7	Order quantity	Quantity discount	Price (each)	Order subtotal	Customer discount	Order total
8	100	0%	$ 15.00	$ 1,500.00	$ 300.00	$ 1,200.00
9	200	5%	$ 14.25	$ 2,850.00	$ 570.00	$ 2,280.00
10	300	7.50%	$ 13.88	$ 4,162.50	$ 832.50	$ 3,330.00
11	400					
12	500					

	A	B	C	D	E	F
1			Customer	Wingtip Toys		
2			Discount	0.2		
3						
4	Product	Toy plane				
5	Base price	15				
6						
7	Order quantity	Quantity discount	Price (each)	Order subtotal	Customer discount	Order total
8	100	0	=$B$5-($B$5*B8)	=A8*C8	=D8*$D$2	=D8-E8
9	200	0.05	=$B$5-($B$5*B9)	=A9*C9	=D9*$D$2	=D9-E9
10	300	0.075	=$B$5-($B$5*B10)	=A10*C10	=D10*$D$2	=D10-E10
11	400	0.1	=$B$5-($B$5*B11)	=A11*C11	=D11*$D$2	=D11-E11
12	500	0.125	=$B$5-($B$5*B12)	=A12*C12	=D12*$D$2	=D12-E12

A mixed reference refers absolutely to either the column or row and relatively to the other. The mixed reference *A$1* always refers to row 1, and *$A1* always refers to column A.

You can reference cells in other worksheets within the workbook. For example, you might prepare a Summary worksheet that displays results based on data tracked on other worksheets. References to cells on other worksheets can be relative, absolute, or mixed.

> **Tip** You can reference a worksheet by whatever name appears on the worksheet tab.

You can also reference cells in other workbooks. For example, you might prepare a report that collates data from workbooks submitted by multiple regional managers.

When referencing a workbook located in a folder other than the one your active workbook is in, enter the path to the file along with the file name. If the path includes a non-alphabetical character (such as the backslash in C:\) in the file name, enclose the path in single quotation marks.

You can refer to the content of a range of adjacent cells. For example, you might use a formula to return the maximum value of all the cells in a row. When referencing a range of cells in a formula, the cell references can be relative, absolute, or mixed.

Drag to select cells   Formula bar   Color-coded cell references

C5			✕ ✓ *fx*	=SUM(C5:C12)			
	A	B	C	D	E	F
1	**Category**	**Name**	**Sales**	**Category Subtotal**		
2	Berry bushes	Blackberries	$31.50			
3	Berry bushes	Gooseberries	$45.00			
4				$76.50		
5	Bulbs	Anemone	$112.00			
6	Bulbs	Autumn crocus	$75.00			
7	Bulbs	Begonias	$37.90			
8	Bulbs	Bulb planter	$13.90			
9	Bulbs	Daffodil	$191.66			
10	Bulbs	Lilies	$56.70			
11	Bulbs	Lily-of-the-Field	$38.00			
12	Bulbs	Siberian Iris	$69.93			
13				=SUM(C5:C12)		
				SUM(**number1**, [number2], ...)		
14	Carnivorous	American Pitcher Plant	$28.00			

➤ **To relatively reference the contents of a cell**

→ Enter the column letter followed by the row number, like this:

A1

➤ **To relatively reference the contents of a range of cells**

→ Enter the upper-left cell of the range and the lower-right cell of the range, separated by a colon, like this:

A1:B3

➤ **To insert a relative reference to a range of cells in a formula**

1. Position the cursor in the location within the formula in which you want to insert the cell range reference.

2. Drag to select the cell range and insert the cell range reference.

➤ **To absolutely reference the contents of a cell**

→ Precede the column letter and row number by dollar signs, like this:

$A$1

➤ **To absolutely reference the contents of a range of cells**

→ Enter the upper-left cell of the range and the lower-right cell of the range, separated by a colon, like this:

$A$1:$B$3

➤ **To reference a cell on a different worksheet in the same workbook**

→ Enter the worksheet name and cell reference, separated by an exclamation point, like this:

Data!C2

Or

1. Click the worksheet tab of the worksheet containing the cell you want to reference.

2. Click the cell or select the cell range you want to reference, and then press **Enter** to enter the cell reference into the formula and return to the original worksheet.

➤ **To reference a cell in another workbook**

→ If the workbook is in the same folder, enter the workbook name in square brackets followed by the worksheet name and cell reference, separated by an exclamation point, like this:

[Sales.xlsx]Data!C2

→ If the workbook is in a different folder, enter the path to the workbook, the workbook name in square brackets, and the worksheet name; enclose all of this in single quotes. Then enter an exclamation point followed by the cell reference, like this:

='C:\PROJECTS\MOS2010\Excel Files\[test.xlsx]Sheet1'!$A$1

Or

1. Open the workbook that contains the cell you want to reference, and then switch to the workbook you want to create the formula in.

2. With the cursor active where you want to insert the reference, switch to the second workbook, click the worksheet containing the cell you want to reference, click the cell or select the range you want to reference, and then press **Enter**.

Defining order of operations

A formula can involve multiple types of calculations. Unless you specify another order of precedence, Excel evaluates formula content and process calculations in the following order:

1. **Reference operators** The colon (:), space ( ), and comma (,) symbols

2. **Negation** The negative (–) symbol in phrases such as –1

3. **Percentage** The percent (%) symbol

4. **Exponentiation** The raising to a power (^) symbol

5. **Multiplication and division** The multiply (*) and divide (/) symbols

6. **Addition and subtraction** The plus (+) and minus (-) symbols

7. **Concatenation** The ampersand (&) symbol connecting two strings of text

8. **Comparison** The equal (=), less than (<), and greater than (>) symbols and any combination thereof

If multiple calculations within a formula have the same precedence, Excel processes them in order from left to right.

You can change the order in which Excel processes the calculations within a formula by enclosing the calculations you want to perform first in parentheses. Similarly, when you use multiple calculations to represent one value in a formula, you can instruct Excel to process the calculations as a unit before incorporating the results of the calculation in the formula, by enclosing the calculations in parentheses.

The following table illustrates the effect of changing precedence within a simple formula.

Formula	Result
=1+2-3+4-5+6	5
=(1+2)-(3+4)-(5+6)	−15
=1+(2-3)+4-(5+6)	−7

➤ **To change the order of calculation within a formula**

→ Enclose the calculations you want to perform first within parentheses.

→ Arrange calculations that have the same precedence in the order you want to perform them, from left to right.

Practice tasks

The practice files for these tasks are located in the MOSExcel2013\Objective4 practice file folder. Save the results of the tasks in the same folder.

- Create a new workbook named *MyReferences*, and complete the following tasks on Sheet 1:
  - In cell A1, enter the formula =*5x2+7-12*.
  - Copy the formula from cell A1 to cells A2:A5. Edit each of the copied formulas, placing parentheses around different groupings to view the effect.

- In the *Excel_4-1a* workbook, on the Practice worksheet, create a formula in cells B2:T20 to complete the multiplication table of the numbers 1 through 20. (Challenge: Create the table in six or fewer steps.) Compare the formulas in your multiplication table to those on the Results worksheet.

- In the *Excel_4-1b* workbook, on the Summary worksheet, display the total sales for each period in cells B2:B5 by referencing the corresponding worksheets.

- In the *Excel_4-1c* workbook, on the Sales By Category worksheet, complete the following tasks:
  - In cells C95, C101, and C104, calculate the sales total for each category by using a relative cell range reference.
  - In cell C86, calculate the Cacti sales total, using an absolute cell range reference.

4.2 Summarize data by using functions

Formulas in Excel can be made up of values that you enter, values that you reference (cell references, named ranges, named objects), mathematical operators, and the functions that ultimately structure and control the formula. A function can be thought of as a service provided by Excel to do a specific task. That task might be to perform a mathematical operation, to make a decision based on specific factors, or to perform an action on some text. A function is always indicated by the function name followed by a set of parentheses. (For example, the SUM() function.) For most functions, arguments (variables) inside the parentheses either tell the function what to do or identify values for the function to work with. An argument can be a value that you enter, a cell reference, a range reference, a named range, a named object, or even another function. The number and type of arguments vary depending on which function you're using. It is important to understand the syntax of common functions and be able to correctly enter the function arguments. Fortunately, you don't have to memorize anything; the Formula AutoComplete feature leads you through the process of selecting the correct function name and entering the required arguments in the correct syntax.

Probably the most common formula used in Excel, and certainly the simplest to understand, is the SUM() function. The SUM() function returns the total value of a set of numbers. Rather than individually adding the values of all the cells you want to total, you can use the SUM function to perform this task.

The following table describes the purpose of each of the functions that you can use to summarize data from a set of cells, and the types of arguments the functions accept.

Function	Purpose	Arguments
SUM()	Returns the total value of the cells	*Number1,Number2,...,Number255*
COUNT()	Returns the number of cells that contain numeric values	*Value1,Value2,...,Value255*
COUNTA()	Returns the number of cells that contain any content (are not empty)	*Value1,Value2,...,Value255*
AVERAGE()	Returns the average of the cell values	*Number1,Number2,...,Number255*
MIN()	Returns the minimum value within the set	*Number1,Number2,...,Number255*
MAX()	Returns the maximum value within the set	*Number1,Number2,...,Number255*

> **Tip** The results of the AVERAGE, COUNT, and SUM functions appear by default on the status bar when you select multiple cells (contiguous or separate) that contain numeric values. You can optionally display the Numeric Count, Minimum, and Maximum values.

Each of these functions takes up to 255 arguments, either numbers or values, as follows:

- An argument specified as a number can be a number that is entered directly in the formula, a text representation of a number (a number inside of quotation marks), a cell reference, a range reference, or a named reference. The function ignores any cells that contain text that can't be translated to a number, that are empty, or that contain an error.

- An argument specified as a value can be any type of value. For example, the COUNT() function will evaluate any type of value and return the count of only those that it identifies as numbers, whereas the COUNTA() function will evaluate any type of value and return the count of all those that are not blank.

You can enter arguments directly in the formula structure, through a dialog box interface, by clicking to select cells, or by dragging to select ranges.

> ➤ **To sum values**

→ In the cell or formula bar, enter the following formula, including up to 255 numbers, which can be in the form of cell references or specific numbers:

=SUM(number1,[number2],[number3]...)

→ On the **Formulas** tab, in the **Function Library** group, click the **AutoSum** arrow (not the button), and then click **Sum**. Select or enter the numeric arguments you want to sum, and then press **Enter**.

→ In the **Function Library** group, click the **AutoSum** button (not the arrow) and press **Enter** to accept the logical range of values selected by Excel (the range immediately above or to the left of the active cell).

→ Click the **AutoSum** button. Click or drag to select the input values you want (press and hold **Ctrl** to select multiple cells and ranges). Then press **Enter**.

Or

1. On the **Formulas** tab, in the **Function Library** group, click **Math & Trig**, and then click **SUM**.

2. In the **Function Arguments** dialog box, do the following, and then click **OK**:

    ○ In the **Number1** box, enter or select the first number.

    ○ In the **Number2** box and each subsequent box, enter or select the additional numbers up to a total of 255 arguments.

> ➤ **To count cells containing numeric values**

→ In the cell or formula bar, enter the following formula, including up to 255 cell references or data ranges:

=COUNT(value1,[value2],[value3]...)

→ In the **Function Library** group, click the **AutoSum** arrow, and then click **Count Numbers**. Select or enter the cells you want to count, and then press **Enter**.

Or

1. In the **Function Library** group, click **More Functions**, click **Statistical**, and then click **COUNT**.

2. In the **Function Arguments** box, do the following, and then click **OK**.

    ○ In the **Value1** box, enter or select the first data range.

    ○ In the **Value2** box and each subsequent box, enter or select additional data ranges up to a total of 255 arguments.

➤ **To count non-empty cells**

→ In the cell or formula bar, enter the following formula, including up to 255 cell references or data ranges:

=COUNTA(value1,[value2],[value3]...)

Or

1. In the **Function Library** group, click **More Functions**, click **Statistical**, and then click **COUNTA**.

2. In the **Function Arguments** box, do the following, and then click **OK**.

   ○ In the **Value1** box, enter or select the first data range.

   ○ In the **Value2** box and each subsequent box, enter or select additional data ranges up to a total of 255 arguments.

➤ **To average values in a data range**

→ In the cell or formula bar, enter the following formula, including up to 255 cell references or data ranges:

=AVERAGE(number1,[number2],[number3]...)

→ In the **Function Library** group, click the **AutoSum** arrow, and then click **Average**. Select or enter the cells you want to average, and then press **Enter**.

Or

1. In the **Function Library** group, click **More Functions**, click **Statistical**, and then click **AVERAGE**.

2. In the **Function Arguments** dialog box, do the following, and then click **OK**:

   ○ In the **Number1** box, enter or select the first data range.

   ○ In the **Number2** box and each subsequent box, enter or select additional data ranges up to a total of 255 arguments.

➤ **To return the lowest value in a data range**

→ In the cell or formula bar, enter the following formula, including up to 255 cell references or data ranges:

=MIN(number1,[number2],[number3]...)

→ In the **Function Library** group, click the **AutoSum** arrow, and then click **Min**. Select or enter the cells you want to evaluate, and then press **Enter**.

Or

1. In the **Function Library** group, click **More Functions**, click **Statistical**, and then click **MIN**.

2. In the **Function Arguments** dialog box, do the following, and then click **OK**:

   ○ In the **Number1** box, enter or select the first data range.

   ○ In the **Number2** box and each subsequent box, enter or select additional data ranges up to a total of 255 arguments.

➤ **To return the highest value in a data range**

→ In the cell or formula bar, enter the following formula, including up to 255 cell references or data ranges:

=MAX(number1,[number2],[number3]...)

→ In the **Function Library** group, click the **AutoSum** arrow, and then click **Max**. Select or enter the cells you want to evaluate, and then press **Enter**.

Or

1. In the **Function Library** group, click **More Functions**, click **Statistical**, and then click **MAX**.

2. In the **Function Arguments** dialog box, do the following, and then click **OK**:

   ○ In the **Number1** box, enter or select the first data range.

   ○ In the **Number2** box and each subsequent box, enter or select additional data ranges up to a total of 255 arguments.

Practice tasks

The practice files for these tasks are located in the MOSExcel2013\Objective4 practice file folder. Save the results of the tasks in the same folder.

- In the *Excel_4-2a* workbook, complete the following tasks on the Summary worksheet:
  - ○ In cell B18, create a formula that returns the number of non-empty cells in the Period range.
  - ○ In cell C18, create a formula that returns the average value in the Sales range.
  - ○ In cell D5, create a formula that returns the lowest Sales value for the Fall period.
- In the *Excel_4-2b* workbook, complete the following tasks on the Sales By Region worksheet:
  - ○ Create subtotals of sales amounts first by *Period* and then by *Region*.
  - ○ Find the average sales by *Period* and then by *Region*.
  - ○ Find the maximum and minimum values by *Period* and then by *Region*.

4.3 Utilize conditional logic in functions

You can use a formula to display specific results when certain conditions are met. To do so, you create a formula that uses conditional logic; specifically the IF() function or one of its variations shown in the following table.

Function	Description
SUMIF() SUMIFS()	Returns the sum of values in a range that meet one or more criteria
COUNTIF() COUNTIFS	Returns the number of cells in a range that meet one or more criteria
AVERAGEIF() AVERAGEIFS()	Returns the average of values in a range that meet one or more criteria

A formula that uses conditional logic evaluates a specific condition and then returns one of two results based on whether the logical test evaluates as TRUE or FALSE.

The correct syntax for the IF() function is as follows:

=IF(logical_test,value_if_true,value_if_false)

> **Tip** The IF() function in Excel is equivalent to an IF...THEN...ELSE function in a computer program.

The logical test and the results can include text strings or calculations. Enclose text strings within the formula in quotation marks. Do not enclose numeric values or calculations in quotation marks.

The syntax for the SUMIF function is *SUMIF(range,criteria,sum_range)*.

The syntax for the COUNTIF function is *COUNTIF(range,criteria)*. For example, the following formula returns the number of students within a table who are in grade 5:

=COUNTIF(AllGirls[[#All],[Grade]],"5")

The syntax for the AVERAGEIF function is *AVERAGEIF(range,criteria,average_range)*.

I12			fx	=COUNTIF(E:E,H12)				
	A	B	C	D	E	F	G H	I
1	Order					Postal	Orders by Region	
2	Date	Name	Address	City	Region	Code	Region	Quantity
3	1/5/2013	Raman Sarin	8808 Backbay St.	Boston	MA	88337	BC	9
4	1/5/2013	Charlie Keen	991 S. Mississippi Rd.	St. Louis	MO	89203	CA	7
5	1/6/2013	George Schaller	401 Rodeo Dr.	Auburn	WA	34923	ID	3
6	1/6/2013	Jed Brown	666 Fords Landing	Westover	WV	66954	MA	1
7	1/8/2013	Patrick Sands	4568 Spaulding Ave. N.	Seattle	WA	12345	MO	1
8	1/12/2013	Andreas Schou	14 S. Elm Dr.	Moscow	ID	02912	MT	2
9	1/12/2013	Bob Kelly	12 Juanita Ln.	Helena	MT	42665	OR	4
10	1/12/2013	Jim Kim	78 Miller St.	Seattle	WA	81233	Québec	1
11	1/12/2013	Eli Bowen	27 Christopher St.	Seattle	WA	67645	UT	1
12	1/13/2013	Colleen Bracy	18 Elm St.	Tulalip	WA	77483	WA	57
13	1/14/2013	Markus Breyer	511 Lincoln Ave.	Burns	OR	27182		
14	1/14/2013	Andy Brauninger	42 El Camino Dr.	Seattle	WA	11299		
15	1/15/2013	Lukas Keller	4220 Main St.	Bellevue	WA	39200		
16	1/16/2013	Thorsten Scholl	89 Cedar Way	Redmond	WA	30293		
17	1/19/2013	Kendall Keil	6778 Cypress Pkwy.	Oak Harbor	WA	30291		
18	1/22/2013	Jennifer Kim	72 West St.	Portland	OR	67823		
19	1/22/2013	Allison Brown	78 Riverside Dr.	Woodinville	WA	27283		

| ◂ ▸ | **Orders** | Details | ⊕ |

READY　　　　　　　　　　　　　　　　　　　　　100%

The criteria is a condition or criteria in the form of a number, expression, or text that defines which cells will be included in the calculation.

> **Tip** You can nest multiple functions so that Excel evaluates multiple conditions before returning a result. You can add logical tests to a conditional formula by using the AND(), OR(), and NOT() functions.

> **Strategy** Nested functions, the multiple-condition formulas SUMIFS(), COUNTIFS(), and AVERAGEIFS(), and custom conditional formats are part of the objective domain for Microsoft Office Specialist Exams 77-427 and 77-428, Microsoft Excel Expert.

➤ **To sum values in a data range that meet a condition**

→ In the cell or formula bar, enter the following formula, where range is the data range you want to evaluate, criteria is the condition that defines which cells will be summed, and sum_range is the data range within which cells will be summed:

=SUMIF(range,criteria,sum_range)

Or

1. On the **Formulas** tab, in the **Function Library** group, click **Math & Trig**, and then click **SUMIF**.

2. In the **Function Arguments** dialog box, do the following, and then click **OK**:
   - In the **Range** box, enter or select the data range you want to evaluate.
   - In the **Criteria** box, enter the condition, in the form of a number, expression, or text, that defines the cells that will be summed.
   - In the **Sum_range** box, enter or select the data range within which you want to sum qualifying cell values. If left blank, the formula sums cells within the data range in the **Range** box.

➤ **To count cells in a data range that meet a condition**

→ In the cell or formula bar, enter the following formula, where range is the data range you want to evaluate and count, and criteria is the condition that defines which cells will be counted:

=COUNTIF(range,criteria)

Or

1. On the **Formulas** tab, in the **Function Library** group, click **More Functions**, click **Statistical**, and then click **COUNTIF**.

2. In the **Function Arguments** dialog box, do the following, and then click **OK**:
   - In the **Range** box, enter or select the data range you want to evaluate.
   - In the **Criteria** box, enter the condition, in the form of a number, expression, or text, that defines the cells that will be counted.

➤ **To average values in a data range that meet a condition**

→ In the cell or formula bar, enter the following formula, where range is the data range you want to evaluate, criteria is the condition that defines which cells will be averaged, and average_range is the data range within which cells will be averaged:

=AVERAGEIF(range,criteria,average_range)

Or

1. On the **Formulas** tab, in the **Function Library** group, click **More Functions**, click **Statistical**, and then click **AVERAGEIF**.

2. In the **Function Arguments** dialog box, do the following, and then click **OK**:

   ○ In the **Range** box, enter or select the data range you want to evaluate.

   ○ In the **Criteria** box, enter the condition, in the form of a number, expression, or text, that defines the cells that will be averaged.

   ○ In the **Average_range** box, enter or select the data range within which you want to average qualifying cell values. If left blank, the formula averages cells within the data range in the **Range** box.

Practice tasks

The practice file for these tasks is located in the MOSExcel2013\Objective4 practice file folder. Save the results of the tasks in the same folder.

- In the *Excel_4-3* workbook, complete the following tasks on the Expense Statement worksheet:

  ○ In cell C25, use the AND function to determine whether the Entertainment total is less than $200.00 and the Misc. total is less than $100.00.

  ○ In cell C26, use the OR function to determine whether the Entertainment total is more than $200.00 or the Misc. total is more than $100.00.

  ○ In cell C27, use the IF function to display the text "Expenses are okay" if the function in C25 evaluates to TRUE and "Expenses are too high" if it evaluates to FALSE.

  ○ In cell C28, use the IF function to display the text "Expenses are okay" if the function in C26 evaluates to NOT TRUE and "Expenses are too high" if it evaluates to NOT FALSE.

  ○ Add 60.00 to either the Entertainment column or the Misc. column to check your work.

4.4 Format and modify text by using functions

You can use the formulas shown in the following table to display text within a cell.

Function	Description
LEFT()	Returns the leftmost character or characters of a text string
MID()	Returns a specific number of characters from a text string, starting at the position you specify
RIGHT()	Returns the rightmost character or characters of a text string
TRIM()	Removes all spaces from text except for single spaces between words
UPPER()	Converts text to uppercase
LOWER()	Converts text to lowercase
CONCATENATE()	Concatenates up to 255 text components into one string

The LEFT(), MID(), and RIGHT() functions count each character in the specified text string The LEFT() and RIGHT() functions take the following arguments:

- **text** (required) The text string to be evaluated by the formula.

- **num_chars** (optional) The number of characters to be returned. If *num_chars* is not specified, the function returns one character.

The syntax for the LEFT() and RIGHT() functions is:

LEFT(text,num_chars)

RIGHT(text,num_chars)

For example, the formula *=LEFT(Students[@[Last Name]],1)* returns the first letter of the student's last name.

The MID() function takes the following arguments:

- **text** (required) The text string to be evaluated by the formula.

- **start_num** (required) The position from the left of the first character you want to extract. If *start_num* is greater than the number of characters in the text string, the function returns an empty string.

- **num_chars** (required) The number of characters to be returned. If *num_chars* is not specified, the function returns one character.

The syntax for the MID() function is:

MID(text,start_num,num_chars)

The MID() function returns selected characters from a text string

The TRIM(), UPPER(), and LOWER() functions each take only one argument: the text string to be processed. The syntax of the functions is:

TRIM(text)

UPPER(text)

LOWER(text)

The CONCATENATE() function can be very useful. Using this function, you can merge existing content from cells in addition to content that you enter in the formula. The syntax for the CONCATENATE() function is:

CONCATENATE(text1, [text2], ...)

For example, this formula returns a result such as *Smith, John: Grade 5*.

=CONCATENATE(Table1[@[Last Name]],", ",Table1[@[First Name]],": Grade ",Table1[@ Grade])

Tip You can use the ampersand (&) operator to perform the same process as the CONCATENATE() function. For example, =A1&B1 returns the same value as =CONCATENATE(A1,B1). The Flash Fill feature performs a similar function.

Strategy Using formulas to format cells is part of the objective domain for Microsoft Office Specialist Exams 77-427 and 77-428, "Microsoft Excel Expert."

➤ **To return one or more characters from the left end of a text string**

→ In the cell or formula bar, enter the following formula, where text is the source text and num_chars is the number of characters you want to return:

=LEFT(text,num_chars)

Or

1. On the **Formulas** tab, in the **Function Library** group, click **Text**, and then click **LEFT**.

2. In the **Function Arguments** dialog box, do the following, and then click **OK**:

   ○ In the **Text** box, enter or select the source text.

   ○ In the **Num_chars** box, enter the number of characters you want to return.

➤ **To return one or more characters from within a text string**

→ In the cell or formula bar, enter the following formula, where text is the source text, start_num is the character from which you want to begin returning characters, and num_chars is the number of characters you want to return:

=MID(text,start_num,num_chars)

Or

1. On the **Formulas** tab, in the **Function Library** group, click **Text**, and then click **MID**.

2. In the **Function Arguments** dialog box, do the following, and then click **OK**:

   ○ In the **Text** box, enter or select the source text.

   ○ In the **Start_num** box, enter the character from which you want to begin returning characters.

   ○ In the **Num_chars** box, enter the number of characters you want to return.

➤ **To return one or more characters from the right end of a text string**

→ In the cell or formula bar, enter the following formula, where text is the source text and num_chars is the number of characters you want to return:

=RIGHT(text,num_chars)

Or

1. On the **Formulas** tab, in the **Function Library** group, click **Text**, and then click **RIGHT**.

2. In the **Function Arguments** dialog box, do the following, and then click **OK**:

   ○ In the **Text** box, enter or select the source text.

   ○ In the **Num_chars** box, enter the number of characters you want to return.

➤ **To convert multiple spaces in a text string to single spaces**

→ In the cell or formula bar, enter the following formula, where text is the source text:

=TRIM(text)

Or

1. On the **Formulas** tab, in the **Function Library** group, click **Text**, and then click **TRIM**.

2. In the **Function Arguments** dialog box, enter or select the source text from which you want to remove extra spaces, and then click **OK**.

➤ **To convert a text string to uppercase**

→ In the cell or formula bar, enter the following formula, where text is the source text:

=UPPER(text)

Or

1. On the **Formulas** tab, in the **Function Library** group, click **Text**, and then click **UPPER**.

2. In the **Function Arguments** dialog box, enter or select the source text that you want to convert to uppercase, and then click **OK**.

➤ **To convert a text string to lowercase**

→ In the cell or formula bar, enter the following formula, where text is the source text:

=LOWER(text)

Or

1. On the **Formulas** tab, in the **Function Library** group, click **Text**, and then click **LOWER**.

2. In the **Function Arguments** dialog box, enter or select the source text that you want to convert to lowercase, and then click **OK**.

➤ **To join multiple text strings into one cell**

→ In the cell or formula bar, enter the following formula, including up to 255 text strings, which can be in the form of cell references or specific text enclosed in quotation marks:

=CONCATENATE(text1,[text2],[text3]...)

Or

1. On the **Formulas** tab, in the **Function Library** group, click **Text**, and then click **CONCATENATE**.

2. In the **Function Arguments** dialog box, do the following, and then click **OK**:

- ○ In the **Text1** box, enter or select the first source text.

- ○ In the **Text2** box and each subsequent box, enter the additional source text.

Practice tasks

The practice file for these tasks is located in the MOSExcel2013\Objective4 practice file folder. Save the results of the tasks in the same folder.

- Open the *Excel_4-4* workbook, and complete the following tasks on the Book List worksheet:

  - ○ In the File By column, insert the first letter of the author's last name.

  - ○ In the Locator column, insert the author's area code.

  - ○ In the Biography column, use the CONCATENATE() function to insert text in the form *Joan Lambert is the author of Microsoft Word 2013 Step by Step, which was published by Microsoft Press in 2013.* (including the period).

Objective review

Before finishing this chapter, ensure that you have mastered the following skills:

4.1 Utilize cell ranges and references in formulas and functions

4.2 Summarize data by using functions

4.3 Utilize conditional logic in functions

4.4 Format and modify text by using functions

5 Create charts and objects

The skills tested in this section of the Microsoft Office Specialist exam for Microsoft Excel 2013 relate to creating charts and objects. Specifically, the following objectives are associated with this set of skills:

5.1 Create charts
5.2 Format charts
5.3 Insert and format objects

You can store a large amount of data in an Excel workbook. When you want to present that data to other people, you might choose to include additional information to help viewers interpret the information. Chapter 2, "Manage cells and ranges," discusses methods for visually interpreting data within the context of a data range or table. You can take that interpretation a step farther by presenting the data in the form of a chart. Using Excel 2013, you can create many types of charts from data stored on one or more worksheets. To simplify the process of choosing a chart type, the Quick Analysis tool recommends charts that are most appropriate for the data you're working with. To aid viewers in interpreting the chart data, you can configure a chart to include identifying elements such as a title, legend, and data markers.

Section 1.3, "Format worksheets and workbooks," discussed methods of inserting graphics in worksheet headers and as backgrounds. You can also enhance the information you present in a workbook by including images such as company logos directly on worksheets, displaying text and graphics in SmartArt business diagrams, and displaying text independent of the worksheet or chart sheet structure within text boxes.

This chapter guides you in studying ways of presenting data in charts and enhancing worksheets by including images, business diagrams, and text boxes.

> **Practice Files** To complete the practice tasks in this chapter, you need the practice files contained in the MOSExcel2013\Objective5 practice file folder. For more information, see "Download the practice files" in this book's Introduction.

5.1 Create charts

Charts (also referred to as *graphs*) are created by plotting data points onto a two-dimensional or three-dimensional axis to assist in data analysis and are therefore a common component of certain types of workbooks. Presenting data in the form of a chart can make it easy to identify trends and relationships that might not be obvious from the data itself.

Different types of charts are best suited for different types of data. The following table shows the available chart types and the data they are particularly useful for plotting.

Chart type	Typically used to show
Area	Multiple data series as cumulative layers showing change over time
Bar	Variations in value over time or the comparative values of several items at a single point in time
Bubble	Correlations between three or more independent items
Column	Variations in value over time or comparisons
Doughnut	Percentages assigned to different components of more than one item
Line	Multiple data trends over evenly spaced intervals
Pie	Percentages assigned to different components of a single item (non-negative, nonzero, no more than seven values)
Radar	Percentages assigned to different components of an item, radiating from a center point
Stock	Stock market or similar activity
Surface	Trends in values across two different dimensions in a continuous curve, such as a topographic map
X Y (Scatter)	Correlations between independent items

You can also create combo charts that overlay different data charts in one space.

To plot data as a chart, all you have to do is select the data and specify the chart type. You can select any type of chart from the Charts group on the Insert tab. You can also find recommendations based on the selected content either on the Charts page of the Quick Analysis tool or on the Recommended Charts page of the Insert Chart dialog box.

> **Tip** The Quick Analysis tool provides access to formatting options that pertain to the currently selected data. From the pages of the Quick Analysis tool, you can apply conditional formatting, perform mathematical operations, create tables and PivotTables, and insert sparklines. Like the Mini Toolbar, the Paste Options menu, and other context-specific tools, the Quick Analysis tool makes existing functionality available in a central location. The reason this is a tool rather than simply a toolbar or menu is that the options shown in the tool—for example, the charts shown on the Charts page—are selected as appropriate for the current data.

If the type of chart you initially select doesn't depict your data the way you want, you can change the type at any time. Most chart types have two-dimensional and three-dimensional variations, and you can customize each aspect of each variation.

Before selecting the data you want to present as a chart, ensure that it is correctly set up for the type of chart you want to create. For example, a pie chart can display only one data series. Select only the data you want to appear in the chart. If the data is not in a contiguous range of rows or columns, either rearrange the data or hold down the Ctrl key while you select noncontiguous ranges.

A chart is linked to its worksheet data, so any changes you make to the plotted data are immediately reflected in the chart. If you want to add or delete values in a data series or add or remove an entire series, you need to increase or decrease the range of the plotted data in the worksheet.

	A	B	C	D	E	F	G	H	I	J	K
1											
2		Jan	Feb	Mar							
3	Allen	$ 7,222	$ 3,878	$ 5,369							
4	Brock	$ 3,008	$ 5,203	$ 7,854							
5	Charles	$ 4,280	$ 7,501	$ 3,951							
6	David	$ 5,098	$ 4,745	$ 1,438							
7	Emma	$ 4,230	$ 3,084	$ 4,549							
8	Frank	$ 6,917	$ 7,717	$ 1,519							
9	Grace	$ 6,979	$ 5,915	$ 6,102							
10	Heather	$ 1,930	$ 1,602	$ 7,400							
11	Irma	$ 8,302	$ 3,441	$ 4,742							
12	Joan	$ 5,656	$ 4,168	$ 2,502							
13	Kay	$ 4,572	$ 6,103	$ 7,129							
14	Linda	$ 5,311	$ 7,380	$ 1,897							
15	Max	$ 1,082	$ 4,404	$ 5,274							
16	Nancy	$ 5,261	$ 4,742	$ 7,706	$ 4,337	$ 4,027	$ 8,021	$ 3,391	$ 7,739	$ 2,909	$ 3,033
17	Olivia	$ 7,030	$ 2,395	$ 1,108	$ 2,310	$ 5,071	$ 8,376	$ 4,728	$ 2,852	$ 5,790	$ 2,232
18	Paul	$ 2,144	$ 5,865	$ 2,192	$ 5,688	$ 6,071	$ 7,697	$ 4,837	$ 4,214	$ 1,660	$ 3,374
19	Quentin	$ 6,264	$ 5,707	$ 6,446	$ 1,257	$ 6,582	$ 4,200	$ 5,286	$ 7,211	$ 3,657	$ 5,553
20	Raina	$ 7,690	$ 5,318	$ 2,905	$ 8,582	$ 5,654	$ 6,927	$ 4,403	$ 6,290	$ 7,362	$ 7,250
21	Steve	$ 2,253	$ 3,384	$ 3,808	$ 2,151	$ 3,262	$ 8,076	$ 6,282	$ 2,610	$ 1,792	$ 6,734
22	Trinity	$ 8,544	$ 7,295	$ 2,119	$ 6,744	$ 7,220	$ 4,523	$ 3,018	$ 6,971	$ 2,172	$ 5,860

Sometimes a chart does not produce the results you expect because the data series are plotted against the wrong axes; that is, Excel is plotting the data by row when it should be plotting by column, or vice versa. You can quickly switch the rows and columns to see whether that produces the desired effect. To see what Excel is doing behind the scenes, you can open the Select Data Source dialog box, in which you can control exactly what is plotted on each axis.

> **Strategy** Practice plotting the same data in different ways. In particular, understand the effects of plotting data by column or by row.

Select Data Source

Chart data range: `=Sales!$A$2:$M$25`

⊞ Switch Row/Column

Legend Entries (Series)

⊞ Add   ✏ Edit   ✕ Remove   ▲ ▼

- ☑ Jan
- ☑ Feb
- ☑ Mar
- ☐ Apr
- ☐ May

Horizontal (Category) Axis Labels

✏ Edit

- ☑ Allen
- ☑ Brock
- ☑ Charles
- ☑ David
- ☑ Emma

Hidden and Empty Cells   OK   Cancel

➤ **To plot selected data as a chart on the worksheet**

→ On the **Insert** tab, in the **Charts** group, click the general chart type you want, and then on the menu, click the specific chart you want to create.

> **Tip** Pointing to a chart type on the menu displays a live preview of the selected data plotted as that chart type.

→ On the **Insert** tab, in the **Charts** group, click **Recommended Charts**. Preview the recommended charts by clicking the thumbnails in the left pane. Then click the chart type you want, and click **OK**.

→ Click the **Quick Analysis** button that appears in the lower-right corner of the selection, click **Charts**, and then click the chart type you want to create.

➤ **To change the type of a selected chart**

1. On the **Design** tool tab, in the **Type** group, click **Change Chart Type**.

2. In the **Change Chart Type** dialog box, click a new type and sub-type, and then click **OK**.

➤ **To modify the data points in a chart**

→ In the linked Excel worksheet, change the plotted values.

➤ **To change the range of plotted data in a selected chart**

→ In the linked Excel worksheet, drag the corner handles of the series selectors until they enclose the series you want to plot.

Or

1. On the **Design** tool tab, in the **Data** group, click **Select Data**.

Or

Right-click the chart border or data area, and then click **Select Data**.

2. In the **Select Data Source** dialog box, do any of the following, and then click **OK**:

   ○ Click the worksheet icon at the right end of the **Chart data range** box, and then drag to select the full range of data you want to have available.

   ○ In the **Legend Entries (Series)** list and **Horizontal (Category) Axis Labels** boxes, select the check boxes of the rows and columns of data you want to plot.

➤ **To plot additional data series in a selected chart**

1. On the **Design** tool tab, in the **Data** group, click **Select Data**.

Or

Right-click the chart border or data area, and then click **Select Data**.

2. In the **Select Data Source** dialog box, at the top of the **Legend Entries (Series)** list, click **Add**.

3. In the **Edit Series** dialog box, in the **Series name** box, enter or select the additional series. If necessary, enter or select the series values. Then click **OK**.

4. In the **Select Data Source** dialog box, click **OK**.

➤ **To switch the display of a data series in a selected chart between the series axis and the category axis**

→ On the **Design** tool tab, in the **Data** group, click the **Switch Row/Column** button.

Or

1. On the **Design** tool tab, in the **Data** group, click **Select Data**.

Or

Right-click the chart border or data area, and then click **Select Data**.

2. In the **Select Data Source** dialog box, click **Switch Row/Column**, and then click **OK**.

Practice tasks

The practice files for these tasks are located in the MOSExcel2013\Objective5 practice file folder. Save the results of the tasks in the same folder.

- In the *Excel_5-1a* workbook, use the data on the Seattle worksheet to plot a simple pie chart.

- In the *Excel_5-1b* workbook, on the Sales worksheet, plot the data as a simple two-dimensional column chart. Then switch the rows and columns.

- In the *Excel_5-1c* workbook, on the Sales worksheet, change the October sales amount for the Flowers category to *888.25*. Then add the November data series to the chart, and change the way the data is plotted so that you can compare sales for the two months.

5.2 Format charts

A chart includes many elements; some required and some optional. The chart content can be identified by a *chart title*. Each data series is represented in the chart by a unique color. A *legend* that defines the colors is created by default, but is optional. Each data point is represented in the chart by a data marker, and can also be represented by a *data label* that specifies the data point value. The data is plotted against an x-axis (or *category axis*) and a y-axis (or *value axis*). Three-dimensional charts also have a z-axis (or *series axis*). The axes can have titles, and gridlines can more precisely indicate the axis measurements.

To augment the usefulness or the attractiveness of a chart, you can add elements. You can adjust each element in appropriate ways, in addition to adjusting the plot area (the area defined by the axes) and the chart area (the entire chart object). You can move and format most chart elements, and easily add or remove them from the chart.

Tip Data labels can clutter up all but the simplest charts. If you need to show the data for a chart on a separate chart sheet, consider using a data table instead.

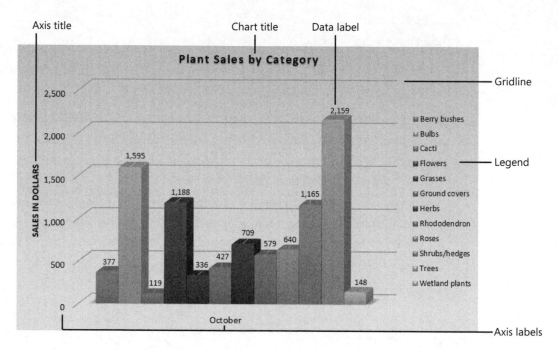

You can add and remove chart elements from the Chart Elements pane or from the Design tool tab.

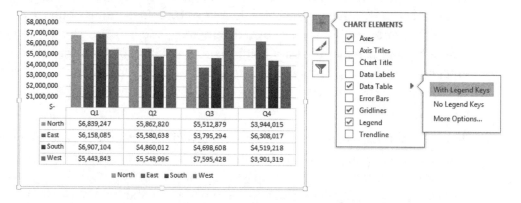

Strategy You can tailor the elements of charts in too many ways for us to cover them in detail here. In addition to choosing options from galleries, you can open a Format dialog box for each type of element. Make sure you are familiar with the chart elements and how to use them to enhance a chart.

By default, Excel creates charts on the same worksheet as the source data. You can move or size a chart on the worksheet by dragging the chart or its handles, or by specifying a precise position or dimensions. If you prefer to display a chart on its own sheet, you can move it to another worksheet in the workbook, or to a dedicated chart sheet.

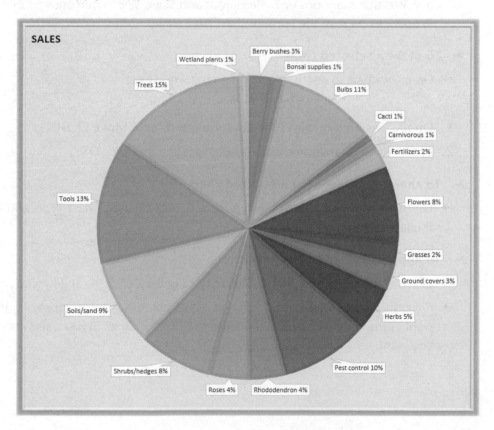

You can apply predefined combinations of layouts and styles to quickly format a chart. You can also apply a shape style to the chart area to set it off from the rest of the sheet.

➤ **To display and hide chart elements**

→ Click the chart, and then click the **Chart Elements** button (labeled with a plus sign) that appears in the upper-right corner of the chart. In the **Chart Elements** pane, select the check boxes of the elements you want to display, and clear the check boxes of the elements you want to hide.

→ On the **Design** tool tab, in the **Chart Layouts** group, click **Add Chart Element**, click the element type, and then click the specific element you want to display or hide.

→ On the **Design** tool tab, in the **Chart Layouts** group, click **Quick Layout**, and then click the combination of elements you want to display.

➤ **To resize a chart**

→ Select the chart, and then drag the sizing handles.

→ On the **Format** tool tab, in the **Size** group, enter the **Height** and **Width** dimensions.

→ On the **Format** tool tab, click the **Size** dialog box launcher, and enter the **Height** and **Width** dimensions or **Scale Height** and **Scale Width** percentages on the **Size & Properties** page of the **Format Chart Area** pane.

➤ **To move a selected chart**

→ Drag the chart to another location on the worksheet.

   Or

1. On the **Design** tool tab, in the **Location** group, click **Move Chart**.

2. In the **Move Chart** dialog box, select a location and click **OK**.

➤ **To change the layout of a selected chart**

→ On the **Design** tool tab, in the **Type** group, click **Change Chart Type**, and then click the layout you want.

➤ **To apply a style to a selected chart**

→ On the **Design** tool tab, in the **Chart Styles** gallery, click the style you want.

→ Click the **Chart Styles** button (labeled with a paintbrush) that appears in the upper-right corner of the chart. On the **Style** page of the **Chart Styles** pane, click the style you want.

➤ **To apply a shape style to a selected chart**

→ On the **Format** tool tab, in the **Shape Styles** gallery, click the style you want.

➤ **To change the color scheme of a selected chart**

→ On the **Design** tool tab, in the **Chart Styles** group, click **Change Colors**, and then click the color scheme you want.

→ Click the **Chart Styles** button that appears in the upper-right corner of the chart. On the **Color** page of the **Chart Styles** pane, click the color scheme you want.

→ Apply a different theme to the worksheet.

> **See Also** For information about applying themes, see section 1.3, "Format worksheets and workbooks."

Practice tasks

The practice files for these tasks are located in the MOSExcel2013\Objective5 practice file folder. Save the results of the tasks in the same folder.

● In the *Excel_5-2a* workbook, on the Sales worksheet, change the pie chart to a 3-D Clustered Column chart. Then apply Layout 1, Style 7, and the Subtle Effect – Accent 3 shape style.

● In the *Excel_5-2b* workbook, on the Sales worksheet, increase the size of the chart until it occupies cells A1:L23. Then move it to a new chart sheet named *Sales Chart*.

● In the *Excel_5-2c* workbook, on the Seattle worksheet, add the title *Air Quality Index Report* to the chart. Then add data labels that show the percentage of the whole that is represented by each data marker. Ensure that the percentages are expressed as whole numbers, with no decimal places.

5.3 Insert and format objects

Although not frequently associated with the storage of data within Excel workbooks, it is worthwhile to note that when preparing to present data, you can incorporate almost all of the graphic elements available in Microsoft Word and PowerPoint into an Excel workbook. This can be particularly useful when creating summary pages or when a workbook must provide a stand-alone information source for text content in addition to data.

> **Tip** You use the same methods to insert and format graphic objects in Excel as you do in other Microsoft Office programs. As an experienced Excel user, you are likely familiar with the methods for inserting, creating, and configuring graphic objects in other programs.

Adding pictures to sheets

The simplest method of enhancing standard workbook content is to add an image, perhaps a company logo, a product image, or an image that represents the concept you want to convey to the workbook viewer. After you insert an image in a document, you can modify it in many ways. For example, you can crop or resize a picture, change the picture's brightness and contrast, recolor it, apply artistic effects to it, and compress it to reduce the size of the document containing it. You can apply a wide range of preformatted styles to a picture to change its shape and orientation, in addition to adding borders and picture effects.

➤ **To insert a picture on a worksheet**

1. On the **Insert** tab, in the **Illustrations** group, click the **Pictures** button.

2. In the **Insert Picture** dialog box, browse to and click the file you want. Then do one of the following:

   ○ Click **Insert** to insert the picture into the worksheet.

   ○ In the **Insert** list, click **Link to File** to insert a picture that will update automatically if the picture file changes.

   ○ In the **Insert** list, click **Insert and Link** to insert a picture that you can manually update if the picture file changes.

➤ **To apply artistic effects to a selected picture on a worksheet**

→ On the **Format** tool tab, in the **Adjust** group, click **Artistic Effects**, and then in the gallery, click the effect you want to apply.

➤ **To apply a style to a selected picture on a worksheet**

→ On the **Format** tool tab, in the **Picture Styles** group, expand the **Quick Styles** gallery, and then click the style you want to apply.

Or

1. On the **Format** tool tab, click the **Picture Styles** dialog box launcher.

2. In the **Format Picture** pane, on the **Fill & Line** and **Effects** pages, choose the options that you want to apply.

➤ **To change the size and/or shape of a selected picture on a worksheet**

→ Drag its sizing handles.

→ On the **Format** tool tab, in the **Size** group, change the **Height** and **Width** settings.

→ On the **Format** tool tab, click the **Size** dialog box launcher. Then on the **Size & Properties** page of the **Format Picture** pane, change the **Height**, **Width**, and **Scale** settings.

➤ **To move a picture on a worksheet**

→ Drag the picture to a new location.

➤ **To copy a picture to a new location on a worksheet**

→ Hold down the **Ctrl** key and drag the picture to the second location.

➤ **To format a selected picture**

→ Use the commands in the **Adjust** group on the **Format** tool tab to remove the picture background; adjust the sharpness, brightness, and contrast; apply artistic effects; and compress the picture to minimize the file size.

→ Use the commands in the **Picture Styles** group on the **Format** tool tab to apply preconfigured combinations of effects or to apply a border, shadow, reflection, glow, soft edge, beveled edge, or three-dimensional effect.

→ Use the commands in the **Arrange** group on the **Format** tool tab to control the relationship of the picture to the sheet and to other pictures on the sheet, and to rotate or flip the picture.

→ Use the commands in the **Size** group on the **Format** tool tab to change the picture height and width and to crop the picture manually, to a specific aspect ratio, to a shape, or to fill or fit a specific space.

Adding text boxes to sheets

To convey information more succinctly, you can add text. When you add text directly to a worksheet, you are restricted by the width and height of the worksheet cells in which you must insert the text. To bypass that restriction, you can insert the text in a text box and position the text box wherever you want it.

➤ **To insert a text box on a worksheet**

1. On the **Insert** tab, in the **Text** group, click **Text Box**.

2. In the worksheet, click to insert a standard-sized text box or drag to draw the text box the size that you want.

3. Enter or paste the text you want to display in the text box.

➤ **To format a selected text box**

→ To change the shape, on the **Format** tool tab, in the **Insert Shapes** group, click **Edit Shape**, click **Change Shape**, and then click the shape you want.

→ To change the shape fill, outline, or effects, on the **Format** tool tab, use the formatting options in the **Shape Styles** group.

→ To rotate the shape, on the **Format** tool tab, in the **Arrange** group, click **Rotate Objects**, and then click the rotation option you want.

→ To change the size of the shape, on the **Format** tool tab, in the **Size** group, modify the height and width, or click the **Size** dialog box launcher and then configure settings in the **Format Shape** pane.

➤ **To format text in a text box**

→ Select the text box. On the **Format** tool tab, use the formatting options in the **WordArt Styles** group.

→ Select the text, and then use the formatting options on the **Mini Toolbar** or in the **Font** group on the **Home** tab.

Adding SmartArt graphics to sheets

To present more complicated information, you can use SmartArt to create a professional business diagram that reflects the thematic elements of your workbook and by doing so, blends in with the rest of the workbook content.

For example, when a worksheet includes details of a process such as a project schedule, you might want to create an accompanying diagram to illustrate the process visually. You can create professional-looking business diagrams by using the SmartArt graphics feature. By using predefined sets of formatting, you can easily create the type of diagram best suited to the worksheet's information. After selecting the type of diagram you want and inserting it into the document, you add text either directly in the diagram's shapes or from its text pane. SmartArt diagrams can consist of only text, or of text and pictures.

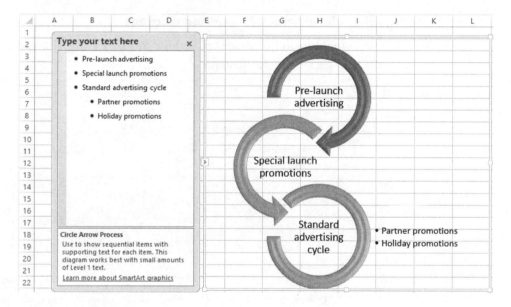

> ➤ **To create a business diagram**
>
> 1. On the **Insert** tab, in the **Illustrations** group, click the **SmartArt** button.
>
> 2. In the left pane of the **Choose a SmartArt Graphic** dialog box, click the type of diagram you want.
>
> 3. In the center pane, click the layout you want, and then click **OK**.

➤ **To apply a style to a selected diagram**

→ On the **Design** tool tab, in the **SmartArt Styles** gallery, click the style you want
to apply.

➤ **To apply a style to a selected diagram shape**

→ On the **Format** tool tab, in the **Shape Styles** gallery, click the style you want to
apply.

Or

1. On the **Format** tool tab, click the **Shape Styles** dialog box launcher.

2. In the **Format Shape** pane, on the **Fill & Line** and **Effects** pages, choose the options
that you want to apply.

➤ **To change the color scheme of a selected diagram**

→ On the **Design** tool tab, in the **SmartArt Styles** group, click the **Change Colors**
button, and then click the color scheme you want.

Practice tasks

The practice file for these tasks is located in the MOSExcel2013\Objective5 practice file folder. Save the results of the tasks in the same folder.

- Open the *Excel_5-3a* workbook, and complete the following tasks:
  - ○ On the Summary sheet, insert the *Excel_5-3b* logo in the upper-left corner.
  - ○ On the Summary sheet, insert a text box on the sheet. Configure the text box to be three inches wide and three inches high, and align it below the heading "Our Prediction." Insert the content of the *Excel_5-3c* text file in the text box. Format the text in 20-point orange Candara font, and center it in the text box.
  - ○ On the Sales worksheet, insert the *Excel_5-3d* product image in cell A1, and configure the content so the product image appears neatly in the space to the left of the sales data.
  - ○ On the Overview worksheet, create a SmartArt graphic of the type Vertical Chevron List that depicts the promotional activity that accompanied each month of sales:

Month	Activity
November	Pre-launch marketing
December	Launch
January	Standard marketing
February	Partner promotions
March	Partner promotions

  - ○ Apply a color set and style to the SmartArt graphic.

Objective review

Before finishing this chapter, ensure that you have mastered the following skills:

5.1 Create charts

5.2 Format charts

5.3 Insert and format objects

Index

Symbols

About the author

 **Joan Lambert** has worked closely with Microsoft technologies since 1986, and in the training and certification industry since 1997. As President of Online Training Solutions, Inc. (OTSI), Joan is responsible for guiding the translation of technical information and requirements into useful, relevant, and measurable training and certification tools.

Joan is a Microsoft Certified Trainer, Microsoft Office Master, Microsoft Certified Technology Specialist, Microsoft Technology Associate, and the author of more than two dozen books about Windows and Office (for Windows and Mac). Joan enthusiastically shares her love of technology through her participation in the creation of books, learning materials, and certification exams. She greatly enjoys communicating the benefits of new technologies by delivering training and facilitating Microsoft Experience Center events.

Joan currently lives in a small town in Texas with her simply divine daughter, Trinity, two slightly naughty dogs, a naturally superior cat, a vast assortment of fish, and the super-automatic espresso machine that runs the house.

Online Training Solutions, Inc. (OTSI)

OTSI specializes in the design, creation, and production of Microsoft Office, SharePoint, and Windows training products for information workers and home computer users. For more information about OTSI, visit *www.otsi.com*.

The team

This book would not exist without the support of these hard-working members of the OTSI publishing team:

- Denise Bankaitis
- Rob Carr
- Susie Carr
- Joyce Cox

- Jeanne Craver
- Kathy Krause
- Marlene Lambert
- Barb Levy

- Jaime Odell
- Victoria Thulman
- Jean Trenary
- Krista Wall

We are especially thankful to the support staff at home who make it possible for our team members to devote their time and attention to these projects.

Rosemary Caperton and Valerie Woolley provided invaluable support on behalf of Microsoft Press.

Now that you've read the book...

Tell us what you think!

Was it useful?
Did it teach you what you wanted to learn?
Was there room for improvement?

Let us know at http://aka.ms/tellpress

Your feedback goes directly to the staff at Microsoft Press,
and we read every one of your responses. Thanks in advance!

 Microsoft